In the footsteps of Jesus

Bishop Edir Macedo

In the footsteps of Jesus

M141
Macedo, Edir, Bishop, 1945 -
   In the footsteps of Jesus / Bishop Edir Macedo ; translated by
Renato Cardoso and Sandra Gouvêa. 2nd ed. - Rio de Janeiro :
Unipro, 2009.
152 p. ; 19,8 cm
Translation from: 'Nos passos de Jesus'.
ISBN 85-7140-278-7 (Brochure)
   1. Christian life - Pentecostal writers. I. Cardoso, Renato,
translation. II. Gouvêa, Sandra, translation. III. Title.
                                                    CDD-248.4

COPYRIGHT © 2006
GENERAL COORDINATION: Sidney S. Costa
EDITORIAL COORDINATION: Renato Cardoso and Mauro Rocha
TEXT LAYOUT: Handerson R. Theodoro and Chris Buddy
ENGLISH VERSION: Renato Cardoso and Sandra Gouvêa
EDITING: David Higginbotham
COVER: Chris Buddy

1st edition 2006
2nd edition 2009

Unipro

Rio de Janeiro
Estrada Adhemar Bebiano. 3.610
Inhaúma – CEP: 20766-720
Rio de Janeiro
Brazil
www.arcauniversal.com
Tel.: + 55 21 3296-9300

Printed and bound in the UK by
J F Print Ltd. Sparkford. Somerset

London
FINSBURY PARK
Rainbow Theatre
232 Seven Sisters Road
Finsbury Park
London N4 3NX
www.uckg.org
Tel.: + 44 (0) 20 7686 6000
Fax: + 44 (0) 20 7686 6008

Index

To my loving sister Elcy
who planted the Seed
in our hearts.

Foreword ▶▶ Foreword ▶▶ Foreword ▶▶

This book played an important part in my conversion when I first read it in 1986. Back then, I knew as much about Jesus as a dentist knows about maritime biology – next to nothing. I was sincere in my desire to follow the Lord, but many questions and doubts made me stumble along the way. What I learned in this book helped me find answers; it also gave me practical teachings that I could immediately apply to my life. The foundation it laid in my heart was key to my spiritual growth, and up to this day I continue to apply the principles and advice that I found in this book.

As you read this, some of you will find yourselves in a situation very similar to mine. You are new to the faith; you have recently begun to attend the church and have been amazed at how little you really know about correctly following Jesus. You want to understand the things of God, but you want to do it right. You want to follow the Lord Jesus very closely and therefore need true, honest, reliable advice from someone who knows.

But some of you are not new to Christianity. You have been following the Lord Jesus for a number of years and may be wondering whether this book will teach you anything you don't already know. There's a chance that it won't, but most probably it will. Some of the things that you will read here are meant to correct, revealing a more effective way of using faith. Be humble and you will learn. Read this book prayerfully, practise what you read, and watch your faith be revived.

Whichever the case, I have no doubt that you will benefit so much from this book that you will find it hard not to pass this copy on to a friend after you're done with it.

May your feet be strong and steady until your journey is complete!

"But he who endures to the end shall be saved."

Matthew 24:13

Bishop Renato Cardoso

Introduction >> Introduction >>

The purpose of this book is to prepare men and women for the spiritual battle that began when they first started believing, and which will continue until the return of the Great King and Lord Jesus Christ.

We have tried to write in straightforward terms so that every reader will be edified on the Rock, and empowered to build up others whom the Lord sends their way as they progress in the greatest goal of life: winning souls for God.

Each one of us has received talents from God – some more than others. But sooner or later, we will be asked to give an account of what we have done with them.

There is a long standing need in the Work of God for workers who are prepared to answer the call to sow the Word in people's hearts. Our Lord Jesus said to His disciples: *"The harvest truly is plentiful, but the laborers are few."* (Matthew 9:37)

Almost two thousand years after those words were spoken, His Church still has the very same need as it considers the vastness of the world, and how few workers are willing to do the Work of God!

For this reason we have written this book, which we hope will give its readers both greater ability and spiritual discernment to develop in the grace and knowledge of the Lord Jesus Christ and His holy will: *"Be diligent to present yourself approved to God, a worker who does not need to be ashamed, rightly dividing the word of truth."* (2 Timothy 2:15)

The author

The origin of chaos

"In the beginning God created the heavens and the earth. The earth was without form, and void; and darkness was on the face of the deep. And the Spirit of God was hovering over the face of the waters."

Genesis 1:1,2

We hope that this book helps you understand why so many people in this world suffer – and cause others to suffer – and how they can find the way out of their problems. In addition, we want to awaken your faith so that you may take advantage of your rights before God the Father, through the name of the Lord Jesus Christ, and by the work and grace of the Holy Spirit.

In the first two verses of Genesis, we find what appears to be a contradiction. The first verse says that God created the heavens and the earth, and the second says that the earth was without form and void. The obvious question is: How could God have created something without form and void? And if so, why? What could His purpose have been?

In reality, the heavens and the earth were as perfect as God Himself when they were first created. That is obvious, since God is not a man, and the work of His hands cannot possibly have flaws or defects. He is limitless; He is Omnipotent, Omnipresent and Omniscient. *"For His name alone is exalted; His glory is above the earth and heaven."* (Psalms 148:13)

Under no circumstances will we ever find any flaw in Him, for it is written:

"Who has measured the waters in the hollow of His hand, measured heaven with a span and calculated the dust of the earth in a measure? Weighed the mountains in scales and the hills in a balance? Who has directed the Spirit of the LORD, or as His counsellor has taught Him? With whom did He take counsel, and who instructed Him, and taught Him in the path of justice? Who taught Him knowledge, and showed Him the way of understanding? Behold, the nations are as a drop in a bucket, and are counted as the small dust on the scales; look, He lifts up the isles as a very little thing. And Lebanon is not sufficient to burn, nor its beasts sufficient for a burnt offering. All nations before Him are as nothing, and they are counted by Him less than nothing and worthless. To whom then will you liken God? Or what likeness will you compare to Him?"

Isaiah 40:12-18

These few verses give only a vague idea of who God really is. Our minds will never be able to grasp the entirety of His Majesty, Power and Glory because our understanding is extremely limited. That is why we sincerely believe that when God created the heavens and the earth they were as perfect as He is.

The events described in the second verse of Genesis must have happened millions of years after the creation of the heavens and the earth. In the interim, the fall of Lucifer occurred, which Ezekiel describes with propriety:

"Moreover the word of the LORD came to me, saying, 'Son of man, take up a lamentation for the king of Tyre, and say to him, "Thus says the Lord GOD: 'You were the seal of perfection, full of wisdom and perfect in beauty. You were in Eden, the garden of God; every precious stone was your covering: the sardius, topaz, and diamond, beryl, onyx, and jasper, sapphire, turquoise, and emerald with gold. The workmanship of your timbrels and pipes was prepared for you on the day you were created. You were the anointed cherub who covers; I established you; you were on the holy mountain of God; you walked back and forth in the midst of fiery stones. You were perfect in your ways from the day you were created, till iniquity was found in you. By the abundance of your trading you became filled with violence within, and you sinned; therefore I cast you as a profane thing out of the mountain of God; and I destroyed you, O covering cherub, from the midst of the fiery stones. Your heart was lifted up because of your beauty; you corrupted your wisdom for the sake of your splendour; I cast you to the ground, I laid you before kings, that they might gaze at you. You defiled your sanctuaries by the multitude of your iniquities, by the iniquity of your trading; therefore I brought fire from your midst; it devoured you, and I turned you to ashes upon the earth in the sight of all who saw you. All who knew you among the peoples are astonished at you; you have become a horror, and shall be no more forever."

Ezekiel 28:11-19

The fall of Lucifer (which means 'full of light') took place between the first and second verses of Genesis, as the prophet Ezekiel describes it. Lucifer was cast down, creating total chaos on earth and making it without form and void.

Note that in the second verse Moses does not say that the heavens were without form and void, but only the earth. That is because the evil cherub and all his followers had been expelled from the heavens. They became the devil (one who separates) and his demons. That is why the heavens remained as they were created while the earth was transformed.

What happened to the earth also happened to man:

"Then God said, 'Let Us make man in Our image, according to Our likeness; let them have dominion over the fish of the sea, over the birds of the air, and over the cattle, over all the earth and over every creeping thing that creeps on the earth.' So God created man in His own image; in the image of God He created him; male and female He created them."

Genesis 1:26,27

"And the LORD God formed man of the dust of the ground, and breathed into his nostrils the breath of life; and man became a living being." (Genesis 2:7) As the earth was created perfect, so was man. Adam was not missing an eye nor did he suffer from any illness. He was created in the image and likeness of the Almighty, and was perfect in every way. Just as Satan (the Hebrew word for 'enemy') entered the earth and made it without form and void, he also entered the life of Adam and Eve. He seduced them in such a way that they stopped listening to God's Word and started listening to his demonic voice.

That is when the great tragedy, chaos and emptiness of humankind began. Man's rebellion against God meant submission to Satan. God is light, order and discipline. Evil, sin and darkness cannot abide with Him. That is why He had no choice but to do to man what He had done to Lucifer: banish him from His presence.

Nature had cooperated with man up to that moment, for he did not have to sweat to eat the fruit of the earth. On the contrary, the earth freely and naturally produced all that man needed because man and earth were siblings by divine creation. But then nature rebelled against man, because man had risen up against its Creator. And today we see how hard man has to struggle to earn his daily bread from the earth, often without success, at times devoured by hunger, misery and misfortune.

Powerless, shrouded in religion, immersed in science, educated and elegant, the world is ruled by satanic principles. Beneath its false appearance is a boiling cauldron of national and international ambition, commercial rivalry, and tears veiled by a smile.

Satan and his hierarchy of evil (Daniel 10:13, Ephesians 6:12) are the invisible agents and the actual force behind the power-hungry, behind the evil minds of dictators and anyone else who uses his temporal power to do evil. Endless wars, death, the shedding of innocent blood and violence accompany them wherever they go.

In the satanic organisation, Satan presides over the fallen spirits that followed him in his first rebellion. His servants give him allegiance and undisputed authority.

When these spirits decided to follow Satan instead of remaining loyal to their Creator, they were irreversibly given over to evil and abandoned in their error. They are in total agreement with their prince and voluntarily offer him service, fulfilling their various duties in a highly organised kingdom (Matthew 12:25). Their initial decision forever bound them to Satan's evil programme and to their inevitable condemnation.

Though Satan's knowledge is both vast and supernatural, it is not a holy or saving knowledge. His demons believe and tremble (James 2:19), but having been given over to evil, they never seek forgiveness and cleansing. They have a clear knowledge that Jesus is Lord of the spiritual world, but this recognition does not involve either a faith that can save or voluntary submission. They respect Christ (Mark 3:11), yet that respect does not derive from a holy communion with Him, but rather from the reluctant surrender of an inferior will to a superior one, with hatred and resentment.

The actions of demonically oppressed people teach us that in some cases demons possess them for purposes of sensual gratification and other impure behaviours. This explains the pleasure that people feel in baring their bodies (Luke 8:27), entertaining evil thoughts and wandering around impure places like graves and burial grounds.

The vicious and vile nature of demons became evident when they revealed their desire to be sent into the swine (Mark 5:13), and when they encouraged free love with the purpose of destroying the morals of an orderly society (Romans 1:24).

In addition to their superhuman intelligence and corrupt morals, they have astonishing powers. They have power over the human body to cause:

- Dumbness (Matthew 9:32,33)

- Blindness (Matthew 12:22)

- Madness (Luke 8:26-36)

- Suicidal thoughts (Mark 9:22)

- Physical illnesses (Mark 9:18)

And all sorts of physical disabilities (Luke 13:11-17) There is no reason to believe that the devil and his angels have ceased their work since the apostles' days. The apostle John wrote that "the whole world lies under the sway of the wicked one." (1 John 5:19)

The original text conveys the idea that "the whole world is asleep under the sleep of the evil one". According to our Lord Jesus Christ, Satan is like a father to those who belong to him. However, he is a merciless father (John 8:44). Satan is also recognised as king and god of this world. His kingdom is a kingdom of darkness and death (Hebrews 2:14; Jude 1:9). An evil spiritual kingdom that works in the children of disobedience, blinding the eyes of their understanding so they will not see the truth of salvation in Jesus Christ (Ephesians 2:2,3; 2 Corinthians 4:3,4; 1 John 3:10; John 12:31; 14:30; 16:11; Acts 26:18).

The devil continues to exert control over unbelievers just as he did over Adam when he sinned. Man's sin and Satan's dominion over man are thus inextricably linked (1 John 3:8). Unbelief and its terrible punishment of eternal condemnation (Mark 16:16) are the consequences of Satan's wicked work in man (Ephesians 2:1,2; 2 Corinthians 4:4; Matthew 13:25). Those who refuse to believe in the Gospel act on Satan's command, who keeps them under his power (Acts 26:18; Colossians 1:13). Denying the existence of demons is itself a consequence of the devil's work in the human heart (2 Corinthians 11:14).

THE ACCUSER AGAINST THE CHURCH OF JESUS CHRIST

The main purpose of Satan is to oppose God's will. The Bible refers to him as:

▶ **Adversary** (Job 1:6-9; Matthew 13:39; Zechariah 3:1; 1 Peter 5:8)

▶ **Devil**, **"accuser"** (Genesis 3:1,5; Job 1:9-11; 2:4,5; Revelation 12:10)

Original sin occurred when Satan's will interfered with God's will, and resulted in the exaltation of himself above all that is called God or that is worshipped (2 Thessalonians 2:4). From Abel's murder to the killing of innocent children by Herod, we clearly see Satan's relentless hatred of the promised seed and his antagonism towards the Messiah of God and the divine purpose to be fulfilled in Him.

We can see the dogged resistance of Satan and his demons to God's plans and purposes in Christ when he personally appeared to tempt the Lord Jesus in the wilderness.

We can also see it in the disturbances he caused in various places, working to frustrate Jesus' public ministry, such as: Judas's betrayal, Peter's denial, and the unbelievable blindness of the Jewish leaders. The same thing can also be seen in Church history, and will continue up until the last and terrible confrontation between God and demons at Armageddon (Revelation 16:13-16).

In the Parable of the Weeds, Jesus spoke about the weeds sown by the devil (Matthew 13:38,39), which the apostle Peter also warned us about in 1 Peter 5:8.

Satan's fury is specifically aimed at the Church of the Lord Jesus Christ:

▶ His demons seek to destroy it by all possible means (Matthew 16:18)

▶ They try to impede listeners from accepting God's Word (Luke 8:12)

▶ They spread false doctrines (Matthew 13:25; 1 Timothy 4:1)

▶ They incite persecution against the Kingdom of God (Revelation 12:7)

No doubt, most of the work is carried out by his messengers and servants – demons. Since Satan is not omnipotent, omnipresent or omniscient, he has to delegate his destructive mission to demons. They, in turn, afflict humankind, altering people's minds through demonic possession (Mark 1:23-27; 5:1-20).

An eternal condemnation of everlasting fire is prepared for Satan and his demons (Matthew 25:41). This is the terrible punishment that the demons were pleading with Jesus about, saying: *"Have You come here to torment us before the time?"* (Matthew 8:29) *"What have we to do with You, Jesus of Nazareth? Did You come to destroy us?"* (Mark 1:24)

Satan will be thrown into the lake of fire and brimstone, his place of eternal condemnation, and will be tormented there, day and night forever and ever (Revelation 20:10).

Satan's demonic partners who collaborated with him in his mission to deceive humankind, will no doubt suffer the same fate at the same time. Every wicked spirit will appear before the white throne for judgement, and will be cast into the eternal flames of Gehenna (Revelation 20:11-15).

The farther away man is from God, the closer he is to the devil. That is why people are suffering the things that we read about and watch on the news. Nobody understands anybody; parents turn against their children and vice-versa; the war of classes; revolutions and wars. Mankind has always struggled, and always will, like vultures fighting over a carcass in the desert. This will continue until the second coming of the Lord Jesus Christ. Hunger, disease, war and all kinds of evil have taken over this world and made it formless and empty all over again...

All the problems afflicting human beings today are due to just one single spark of destruction: man's rebellion against God, his Creator. The spiritual stupidity of man has stopped him from listening to God's Word so that he will listen to the devil, and for this reason, he remains in suffering and pain. Man reaps today what he sowed yesterday; and will reap tomorrow what he sows today. His life is in his hand, though he foolishly does not realise it. As long as he walks with the devil, he will continue to suffer the consequences of his rebellion against God.

The devil, formerly Lucifer, 'slipped up' in spite of all his wisdom. Now he tries to cause man to make the same mistake and be separated from his Creator.

In the face of all this, what can we do to escape the destruction that grips the world today? What can we do to get back to the Garden of Eden and find communion with God? Is there any hope for us?

Our Lord Jesus Christ promised us an abundant life. In the following pages, you will find the path to a truly abundant life, here and now, and in the world to come, eternal life!

Ten steps to salvation

Many people who used to be addicted to drugs, involved in demonic activities, have attended our meetings – people who were lost and hopeless in this world. Today, after having attended our deliverance services and followed these ten steps to salvation, they are completely free. Their lives have changed, they are filled with the presence of the Holy Spirit, and are now faithfully helping us in the Work of the Lord.

STEP ONE: Truly accept the Lord Jesus as the only Saviour – Accepting Jesus as Lord and Saviour is much more than a simple, intellectual decision. To "accept", in the biblical sense, means to believe, trust and follow. Many say they have accepted Jesus; however, they maintain their belief in other gods and have failed to place their faith totally in Him. They say they accept Jesus, but they also say "all religions lead to God." They submit to spirits and idols and put their trust in them. They say God is good, but the devil is not too bad. They act exactly as Satan wants them to.

Such people will not be delivered as long as they be-have this way because God is not a god of confusion. A true follower of Jesus cannot waver between yes and no; he cannot hesitate between two different thoughts. Such indecision is unacceptable in God's eyes. No one can dwell in both light and darkness at the same time, because either the light will drive away the darkness, or the darkness will smother the light.

Accepting Jesus Christ entails abandoning our old life, turning away from evil, submitting to the Lord Jesus through His Word, denying ourselves, taking up our cross and following Him. If a person actually does this, he is ready to overcome anything. A thousand problems may come, yet the true Christian will prevail. His struggle may be against the entire world – but even that will not be too difficult for him.

Imagine yourself in a stormy sea where your boat is sinking and there is nothing around for you to grab hold of. Suddenly, someone comes along in a large boat and stretches out his hand. You would naturally grab hold of that hand even before you knew whose hand it actually was. You would be forever grateful to that person, who in a moment of despair, when death was all around, rescued you and saved your life. This is what the Lord Jesus does for us. Though we may not know Him well, His hand is out-stretched to save us from death. Accept Him as Saviour – His hand is outstretched to release you from all evil, and to give you total freedom.

STEP TWO: Regularly attend meetings for deliverance – Participation in our meetings of deliverance is very important for those who sincerely want to have a new life, far from the influence of evil spirits.

Certain demons do not leave a person's life just because he or she attended a service in the church. Some catch people when they are out in the street or even in their homes. In some cases, a person may be disputed by hundreds of demons who fight to possess him.

Be aware that the devil will never accept defeat in battle. He will always seek revenge and look for a way to crawl back into a person's life. This is one of the main reasons why regular participation in the church's deliverance meetings is so important for those who want total freedom.

STEP THREE: Seek the baptism in the Holy Spirit – Man was designed by God to be the temple of the Holy Spirit. Yet, because of his rebellion, man gives the control of his body, mind and soul over to evil spirits. However, the Lord is ready to give His Spirit to those who seek Him.

The baptism in the Holy Spirit can be seen as the second blessing, for it normally occurs soon after a person is saved. After surrendering your life to Jesus and being set free, you should diligently seek this baptism.

STEP FOUR: Walk in holiness – The word "holy" means, in its simplest definition, "separate". No one can expect to be free from Satan and his demons if he obeys his own will. Those who wish to serve God must live according to His will. John says that the man who is in Christ must walk just like Jesus walked; therefore, a person who wants to follow Jesus must behave in a holy and blameless way.

If you really want salvation, sever all ties with the devil, hold your head up high, be unashamed and, by your own choice and will, submit yourself to God.

STEP FIVE: Read the Bible every day – *"Your word is a lamp to my feet and a light to my path."* (Psalms 119:105)

It is impossible to have perfect communion with God without knowing His holy will. When Jesus triumphed over the devil, He did it using the Word of God, which is the sword of the Holy Spirit. When we use it with faith, nothing in this world can defeat us. It has the power to reach into our innermost parts, separating soul and spirit, joints and marrow. When a servant of God uses it in the name of the Lord Jesus, it produces extraordinary results.

Whoever wants to defeat Satan must be very familiar with God's Word, the Holy Bible. The centurion said to the Lord Jesus that just one word from His mouth could heal his servant. And so it happened! That word reached the centurion's servant and performed the miracle. Through this wonderful Word, great miracles are still happening. God's Word stirs up faith in our hearts so that we can resist the devil; that is why we must know it well.

STEP SIX: Avoid bad company – Experience has taught us that one of the main steps to freedom and salvation is to avoid ties with those who are not in the same faith. There is a saying that goes, "A man is known by the friends he keeps." Indeed, we have ample reasons to consider this an important step to a person's salvation and to include it in this list.

Many people start off in a very promising way in the church, only to give up after a while because of bad friendships.

You should make friends with people of the same faith and avoid, at all costs, gossip, arguments or any other contacts that might jeopardise your salvation.

STEP SEVEN: Be baptised in water – The blessings of God are promised to those who believe and are baptised – something that must happen immediately after a person has accepted Jesus Christ as his personal Saviour. Baptism in water brings death to the works of the flesh; it is the burying of the old self and the birth of a new creature – clean and washed, ready for a new life.

After accepting Jesus as our Saviour, we must not allow bad habits or any other work of the flesh to disturb our relationship with the Lord. Foul moods, pride, selfishness, etc, are works of the flesh and must be left behind. How can we be born again unless we first die? We cannot contain two natures inside ourselves, one sinful and the other converted. To die with Christ means that our flesh cannot bear any more fruit. We have to live in obedience to the Holy Spirit, in newness of life.

STEP EIGHT: Attend the meetings for members – Without a doubt every new convert needs the proper guidance to stay on the path of true Christianity. Church meetings, where members come together to worship the Lord and hear His Word, are like cool water for a thirsty Christian. We need to feed our faith with the Word of truth, which is our weapon against the traps of Satan.

STEP NINE: Be faithful in tithes and offerings – When a person decides to follow the Lord Jesus, he has to live in accordance with His rules. Being His follower involves carefully listening to His voice.

The Bible says in Malachi 3:10 that there is a devouring spirit behind the misery, misfortune and chaos in the lives of those who rob the Lord in tithes and offerings.

When God created man, He not only made him perfect, but He placed him over all of His creation. Man was given the right and privilege of ruling the earth; however, God demanded a tenth of all the fruit of his labour. He did this, among other reasons, to provide a way for us to recognise Him as Lord of all things, and to acknowledge that we are His servants.

If we are faithful to God, the Creator of all things, He will certainly be faithful to us and never allow us to lack anything. Nor will He allow devouring spirits to attack us.

God is glorified with the firstfruits of our income. Besides, 90% of your salary with God is worth much more than 100% of your salary without God's protection. When a person gives tithes and offerings it means that he truly loves God's Work and is concerned about keeping it going.

"'Bring all the tithes into the storehouse, that there may be food in My house, and try Me now in this,' says the LORD of hosts, 'If I will not open for you the windows of heaven and pour out for you such blessing that there will not be room enough to receive it. And I will rebuke the devourer for your sakes, so that he will not destroy the fruit of your ground, nor shall the vine fail to bear fruit for you in the field', says the LORD of hosts."

Malachi 3:10,11

STEP TEN: Watch and pray without ceasing – You may think this step is too difficult, but it is vital to your complete deliverance. To pray without ceasing is to live in a continual spirit of prayer, to be permanently in touch with God. How often do you find yourself talking to someone and at the same time asking God, in spirit, for the solution to their problems?

Our hands may be tied, but our spirit can be linked to God. This step obviously includes personal prayers, group prayers with other faithful friends, prayers on our knees, etc. We will not be deceived, and Satan will never find a way to squeeze into our lives, as long as we watch and pray without ceasing.

The Bible affirms that the devil is continually prowling around, roaring like a lion, in the hope of catching those who are spiritually asleep. When we are watching and praying, not only does the devil keep his distance, but he is also made to bow down to our prayers. No demon can stand the power of God in the lives of those who constantly pray and keep watch in the presence of God.

Knowledge of the Word

God will never endorse a person as an 'approved worker' as long as he has no knowledge of His Holy Word. It is written: *"Your word is a lamp to my feet and a light to my path."* (Psalms 119:105)

As soon as a person finds salvation through the Lord Jesus Christ, he will begin to feel a strong desire to share this same blessing with others who are lost in the world. Compelled by the Holy Spirit, this new Christian will begin his personal ministry of winning souls for God's kingdom.

We all know that we have to work to earn our daily bread, and that it is achieved only through the sweat of our brow. In the same way, in order to achieve something for the Work of God, our hearts have to 'sweat' before the Lord, seeking His holy will for our lives. And this is possible only through knowledge of the Holy Scriptures.

When a person sets out to win souls, he must be conscious of one thing: he will upset the spiritual forces of evil. His struggle will no longer be fought on a physical battlefield; it is now to be fought exclusively in the spiritual realm. He will have to fight against the spirits that rule this dark world and, in order to succeed, he will need to have a rich knowledge of God's Word, for it is the only available weapon with the power to triumph over demons.

"For the word of God is living and powerful, and sharper than any two-edged sword, piercing even to the division of soul and spirit, and of joints and marrow, and is a discerner of the thoughts and intents of the heart."

Hebrews 4:12

With the aim of making Christians fully equipped, the apostle Paul gives a description of the armour of God (Ephesians 6:10-18). In this passage, he refers to the Word of God as the sword of the Holy Spirit. Christians need to be familiar with this Word in order to use it against the evil forces. In fact, the Lord Jesus Himself used solely the Word of God to overcome temptation in the wilderness. And it is interesting to note that Satan resorted to using God's Word to tempt Jesus when he saw Jesus' tactic. However, the Lord Jesus used the Word once more to defeat him (Matthew 4:1-11).

The Lord Jesus' victory in the temptation was due to the words "It is written", followed by a quote from the Scriptures.

Time and again, we see the effectiveness of the Word of God when praying for people in distress. I remember once praying for a heavy-set girl who was possessed by a legion of demons. I prayed using the name of Jesus over and over again, and yet she continued to be possessed. I was physically exhausted, almost at the end of my strength, but then I quoted a verse from the Word of God and ordered the demons to leave her body forever in the name of our Lord Jesus Christ. At that same moment, she was finally released from the demons.

Simply using the name of Jesus is not always effective. It is at times necessary to quote a passage from the Bible so that the demons involved can see that the person confronting them has a real knowledge of the rights given to him by the Lord Jesus.

The devil needs to see that he is not dealing with an amateur who is just playing around, using the situation to show off. We must show Satan that we are the people of God, and that the Lord Jesus Christ has given us a means of defence against demons; that we are fully aware of our responsibilities and authority as described in the promises of our Lord Jesus, which we keep in our hearts. Therefore, we encourage everyone to read the Bible in its entirety.

How to read the Bible

Many people get discouraged when reading the Bible because they rarely understand what they are reading. Others get lost in the genealogies and numbers of the Old Testament. Despite that, *"all Scripture is given by inspiration of God, and is profitable for doctrine, for reproof, for correction, for instruction in righteousness."* (2 Timothy 3:16)

Therefore, it does not matter how difficult, complicated or even tiring your study of the Scriptures might be. It is the Word of God, and what you do not understand today will become clear tomorrow. The important thing is that you get to know it, because sooner or later it will be crucial in solving your problems.

You should not be disappointed when you do not understand certain parts of the Bible. There has never been a man in the world capable of understanding the entire thing. In fact, this is why there are so many different church denominations in this world. Each one interprets the Bible in its own way.

Here are some useful tips on how to effectively read the Bible:

▶ Before you read the Bible, make a sincere prayer to the Holy Spirit, and ask Him for light and guidance in your reading.

▶ It is a good idea to read three chapters of the Old Testament and two of the New Testament every day.

▶ Choose a quiet place where you can read in peace. You should read in a seated position, never lying down.

▶ Never read the Bible in a hurry. On the contrary, read it slowly, taking note of the punctuation, which is a very important aid to understand what is written.

▶ Pay attention to the verbs because they express action.

▶ Take note of the words you do not understand, and after your reading, look them up in a dictionary.

▶ Keep on reading, even if you do not understand a particular section very well. When you read those passages at a later time, they will be clearer to you.

▶ Never put off the chapters that you should read today until tomorrow. Remember that the devil will try everything he can to make you give up on reading the entire Bible, because he knows that if you do, you will be better equipped and stronger in your faith.

The only way to stimulate faith in ourselves and in those around us is to read and explain passages of the Bible. Personal testimonies, however good they may be, will never be as effective as the Word of God. When we give personal testimonies, it should be for the purpose of encouraging and motivating our hearers to seek the solution to their problems in God, through prayer. Only by speaking the Word of God will we be able to awaken people's faith.

"So then faith comes by hearing, and hearing by the word of God." (Romans 10:17)

Many Christians are publicly ridiculed for misquoting the Bible. For instance, I once heard a person say that the Holy Spirit came upon the disciples as a wind. In fact, the Spirit came upon the disciples, and the sound of it was *like* the sound of a mighty wind.

From this small example we can see the great need of having real knowledge of the Word of God, as the apostle Paul said, *"Be diligent to present yourself approved to God, a worker who does not need to be ashamed, rightly dividing the word of truth."* (2 Timothy 2:15)

If you really want to grow in the grace and knowledge of our Lord Jesus Christ and become a vessel chosen by God, you must pay special attention to your spiritual life and make the effort to grow in the Word of God. His Word is the one and only support for our faith.

The Word of God is so important that the Bible contains an entire psalm devoted to exalting its virtues in every single verse: Psalm 119. The Lord Jesus Himself said, *"Heaven and earth will pass away, but My words will by no means pass away."* (Mark 13:31)

When Queen Elizabeth II was being crowned in Westminster Abbey, she was given a Bible during the ceremony. While handing it to her, the church minister said, "Our gracious Queen, we present you with this Book, the most valuable thing that this world affords." A royal present indeed. Truly, it is the most precious thing that could ever be given, for it is the fruit of God's inspiration.

SAVING WISDOM

Those who sincerely search for the truth must never give up reading the Bible. There is a saving wisdom in the

Bible that is not found in any other book. Christianity is not based on a mere book, but on a Living Person. The Scriptures "testify of Me", said Jesus in John 5:39. The only place where we can find direct knowledge of this Person and His teachings is the Bible.

FIRST: The Scriptures are profitable for doctrine – The Word prepares us for life. When we look at it through the eyes of God, we see that the Word of God educates and teaches the way of true life in Christ. It is impossible for the church to exist without the revelation of the Word of the Lord through the Bible. His Word gives us wisdom for life. It is an educational tool of God's Grace. It teaches us how to live, as Titus said, *"Teaching us that (…) we should live soberly, righteously, and godly in the present age."* (Titus 2:12)

SECOND: The Scriptures are profitable for reproof – This means that they are useful in making us see what is wrong in life. They are invaluable in convincing us of wrong and revealing the right way to live.

The Bible causes man to see his fallen condition before God and before life itself. By the action of the Spirit, the Bible leads him to conversion and guides him to Christ and to a more abundant life in Him.

It is impossible to count how many people have experienced such a transformation in their lives. The Scriptures have revealed the way of getting to God to men and women everywhere because there is saving wisdom within its words – wisdom that comes from God. No other book is capable of changing alcoholics, prostitutes, sexual perverts, thieves, murderers, addicts and criminals into kind, God-fearing and productive members of society.

THIRD: The Scriptures are useful for correction – Everything in life – ideas, opinions, behaviour, teachings, theories, theology, ethical values, etc. – must be tried and tested against the teachings of the Bible. If they oppose its basic principles, they must be rejected. The Word of God is capable of not only scrutinising ideas, but also of providing guidance that corrects the life of a person, a nation or, indeed, the world.

We must all develop our intellectual abilities to enquire, learn and speculate. However, everything must be seen in the light of Christ and be tested against the testimony of the Scriptures.

If people really do this, drastic changes will occur in their lives, homes, social groups, relationships, even in national and international relations.

The divine revelation of Christ brings man face to face with his Creator; his self-importance is rendered meaningless. Jesus breaks down the barriers which we have built around ourselves, using His Word as a corrective tool.

Fourth: The Holy Scriptures are profitable for instruction in righteousness – The Bible develops a fundamental sense of justice within each one of us, and motivates us to do good works, for which we were created. His divine Word educates mankind in the ways of justice, which is one of the rarest of virtues in modern life, and achieves this solely through the light of God's Word, whose final revelation is Christ.

History tells us that Frederick the Great, the King of Prussia, wanted to extend his garden. On one side was a miller's property. Emissaries from the palace went to the modest owner of the mill, telling him of the king's need for his land, and asking him how much he wanted to be paid for it. The miller answered that he would not sell the property because it belonged to him, just as surely as the country of Prussia belonged to the king. Frederick then called him in and did his very best to buy the mill. The miller replied that his grandfather had died there and that all his children had been born there. He would not sell it at any price. Losing his temper, the powerful monarch shouted:

"Do you not know that I have the power to take away your land without paying you a penny?"

"You could, if there was no justice." – answered the mill owner.

Delighted with his answer, Frederick said to the miller:

"Neighbour, keep your land."

One century later, the miller's great-grandson had terrible financial problems and sent word to the ruler at the time that he was interested in selling the mill. The king, Frederick's descendant, sent him the following message:

"Dear neighbour, the mill is neither yours nor mine. It belongs to history. It is therefore impossible for me to buy it from you or for you to sell it to me. But since all neighbours must help each other, I am sending you a payment order which you can withdraw at the royal treasury."

Now that many centuries have passed, that mill is probably long gone, but this event will remain in history as an everlasting symbol of the sense of justice that should live in the hearts of great men.

God is just. His Word guides us on our way to a new life, where real justice exists in man's relationship with God, among people themselves, and among social groups and nations. The Bible is the source of justice, which translates into a new way of life and of relationships.

We should study it not only for our own personal edification, but also in order to be used by God to save other people, to comfort and to awaken people to justice. God calls us to live responsibly and sensibly with our neighbours.

4

Prayer

Prayer is the most effective way to communicate with God. Only through prayer can our communion with the Lord Jesus Christ be maintained.

When we make a sincere and honest prayer, we open our hearts to the Lord. This is the prayer 'in spirit and in truth' that the Bible talks about. When we pray this way, we have a better understanding of what our deepest needs are and how much we depend on God. In addition, we develop greater spiritual strength, which guarantees our victory over temptation.

Since prayer is an expression of our soul to the Creator, it does not need to be refined and sophisticated, or marked by long and difficult words. God knows every detail of who we are and what we are asking – so prayer should be simple and objective, and made in a very humble way.

Prayer is effective, that is, it is answered, only when we pray with the absolute assurance that God hears us when we call upon Him. If we do not have this assurance when we are praying, then our words are a waste of time. For this reason, the place we choose to pray must be a place where we can concentrate, making it easier to be wholehearted in what we are doing.

When Jesus taught the Lord's Prayer to His disciples, He did not intend for us to say it verbatim whenever we wanted to speak to God. On the contrary, He was simply leaving a model of how we should communicate with our Heavenly Father.

CHARACTERISTICS OF PRAYER

There are many aspects to prayer, but basically, we can divide them into three different parts:

1 – Worship

2 – Request

3 – Thanksgiving

WORSHIP – Worship is essential to entering into the presence of God in prayer. As we praise, honour and magnify our Lord in an ever-increasing manner, our humility deepens and the sincerity of our soul shines through. When we enter into the presence of God through worship, we are acknowledging His Holiness.

Here are some examples of effective prayer:

◗ Hezekiah's prayer (2 Kings 19:14-19)

◗ Elijah's prayer (1 Kings 18:36)

◗ David's prayer (Psalms 8)

- The Lord's Prayer (Matthew 6:9-13)

- The prayer of the Primitive Church (Acts 4:24-31)

- The leper's prayer (Matthew 8:2)

- The prayer of the Canaanite woman (Matthew 15:22)

- The prayer of Jairus (Mark 5:22,23)

Worship is present at the beginning of each one of these prayers.

There is no perfect man in this evil world. Even so, those who consider themselves inferior honour their 'superiors'. For example, judges are addressed as "Your Honour"; kings are called "Your Majesty"; other members of royalty are called "Your Highness"; some are even called "Your Lordship." Bearing this in mind, we should all the more enter into God's presence with as much honour, glory and praise as we can possibly evoke, for He – and only He – is worthy of all praise!

Worship can also cause extraordinary miracles to happen in our lives. That is what happened to the apostle Paul and Silas when they were in chains and in jail. They began to pray and sing praises to God while their fellow prisoners listened. Suddenly, at around midnight, a violent earthquake shook the foundations of the prison. All the prison doors flew open and everyone's chains fell off (Acts 16:24-26).

In truth, praise is the food of God. Just as the sweet perfume of flowers attracts bees, our praise and worship, like incense, draws God closer to us. Therefore, before speaking about what we want, we should draw His attention through praise.

REQUEST – Immediately prior to teaching the Lord's Prayer, Jesus said, *"For your Father knows the things you have need of before you ask Him."* (Matthew 6:8)

God no doubt knows all of our requests before we ever ask Him. And yet, it is necessary to ask, because asking awakens our faith as we seek more intimate contact with God. When our prayers are answered, we glorify our Lord even more. So, the more we ask, the more we receive, and the more we glorify the Lord. This is what our Lord Jesus meant when He said, *"And whatever you ask in My name, that I will do, that the Father may be glorified in the Son."* (John 14:13)

This means that our requests serve to glorify God the Father through our Saviour Jesus.

What we can and cannot ask – Our requests have no meaning to God unless they have a clear objective. We have to ask ourselves whether what we want will bring glory to God or if it will simply be used to satisfy our lusts, and cause an even greater separation between Him and us.

James exhorts us about this, saying, *"Where do wars and fights come from among you? Do they not come from your desires for pleasure that war in your members? You lust and do not have. You murder and covet and cannot obtain. You fight and war. Yet you do not have because you do not ask. You ask and do not receive, because you ask amiss, that you may spend it on your pleasures. Adulterers and adulteresses! Do you not know that friendship with the world is enmity with God? Who-ever therefore wants to be a friend of the world makes himself an enemy of God."*

James 4:1-4

How often do we insist with God about something we want, thinking that it is right for us, only to wish that we had never asked for it when we finally receive it?

All of our requests to God must be in accordance with the Scriptures and be subject to the will of God. For instance, the healing of a disease is the will of God because the Holy Scriptures state as much, and because Jesus confirmed it by healing all who came to Him. Blessed finances are a promise of both God the Father and the Lord Jesus (Malachi 3:10; John 10:10). It is also the will of God for us to have and enjoy spiritual peace. In short, we can ask God for anything in the following categories:

◗ Physical blessings – divine healing

◗ Financial blessings – an abundance of material needs

◗ Spiritual blessings – eternal salvation in Jesus Christ

◗ Many people spend their entire lives asking for a certain blessing and never receive it. Why is that? Thousands of blessings are promised in the Bible. If we do not specify exactly what it is that we want, our Lord is unable to give it to us. If we want a better salary, we have to tell Him, "My Lord, I want a monthly salary of X." If we want a new car, we have to tell Him specifically what model and make – and so on. We need to know how to ask in order to receive!

THANKSGIVING – I believe it is unnecessary to say much about this important part of prayer because gratitude is the natural expression of those who have received God's blessing. But when we thank our Lord even before we receive the answer, we are offering solid proof of a true faith in Him.

I must add that none of what has been explained about prayer so far will have any effect if we do not use the key that unlocks every answer to prayer: the name of the Lord Jesus Christ. Jesus said, *"And whatever you ask in My name, that I will do, that the Father may be glorified in the Son."* (John 14:13)

God the Father answers our requests because of the name of His Son Jesus. This name is the secret behind every miracle!

Forgiveness

Anyone wanting to follow in the footsteps of the Lord Jesus cannot afford to ignore one of the most important moral laws: forgiveness. Christianity would not survive, nor would the coming of our Lord Jesus make any sense, if the spirit of forgiveness were not at work in human hearts.

The Bible teaches us that God understands our failings, our mistakes and our weaknesses, but He cannot tolerate a person who refuses to forgive. Those who refuse to forgive are being dishonest with themselves, for everybody makes mistakes. Those who forgive will be shown mercy by God and men, while those who are inflexible will have no hope of being saved!

When we cling to resentment against a person, evil is planted in our hearts and begins to grow; the longer it is allowed to stay there, the more difficult it will be to uproot it. Attempting to forget it or even repress it with good works is useless, because sooner or later its foliage and bad fruit will appear. This is why we say that forgiveness is much more than a virtue – it is a need.

The Bible is filled with instances of how God reacts to mankind's sins and mistakes.

Throughout His ministry, the Lord Jesus was an example of how to behave towards others. The miracles He performed revealed His mercy towards sinners. We should follow His example.

"Therefore the kingdom of heaven is like a certain king who wanted to settle accounts with his servants. And when he had begun to settle accounts, one was brought to him who owed him ten thousand talents. But as he was not able to pay, his master commanded that he be sold, with his wife and children and all that he had, and that payment be made. The servant therefore fell down before him, saying, 'Master, have patience with me, and I will pay you all.' Then the master of that servant was moved with compassion, released him, and forgave him the debt. But that servant went out and found one of his fellow servants who owed him a hundred denarii; and he laid hands on him and took him by the throat, saying, 'Pay me what you owe!' So his fellow servant fell down at his feet and begged him, saying, 'Have patience with me, and I will pay you all.' And he would not, but went and threw him into prison till he should pay the debt. So when his fellow servants saw what had been done, they were very grieved, and came and told their master all that had been done. Then his master, after he had called him, said to him, 'You wicked servant! I forgave you all that debt because you begged me. Should you not also have had compassion on your fellow servant, just as I had pity on you?' And his master was angry, and delivered him to the torturers until he should pay all that was due to him. So My heavenly Father also will do to you if each of you, from his heart, does not forgive his brother his trespasses."

Matthew 18:23-35

This parable illustrates the difficult law of forgiveness, which has to be practised by every follower of the Lord Jesus Christ, no matter the cost! This teaching reveals that a person cannot take possession of the Kingdom of Heaven as long as he holds a grudge against his neighbour. In the model of prayer the Lord Jesus taught us, He says, *"And forgive us our debts, as we forgive our debtors."* (Matthew 6:12)

If we want God's amazing forgiveness, we must forgive others. Even when people's mistakes are huge, they will seem small and insignificant in comparison to our many sins against God the Father, God the Son and God the Holy Spirit.

It is the continual duty of every Christian to love and forgive his enemies. God Himself is our greatest example of forgiveness: He, through Christ, forgave mankind, who did not deserve to be forgiven.

Here, the Lord Jesus Christ is teaching us how to treat a "brother" who offends us. In this particular case, the word brother refers to a brother in faith, not simply a blood brother. No doubt it referred to reconciliation between Jews when it was taught for the first time; however, this teaching is still in force today and is the guide for anyone who wants to be reconciled with another person.

In Matthew 18:21,22, the teaching is so incisive that many Christians would like to ignore it. In verse 21 Peter asks: *"Lord, how often shall my brother sin against me, and I forgive him? Up to seven times?"* Peter knew he had to forgive his brother, but he had hoped that there would be a limit to this forgiveness.

How many modern-day Christians would also like to put limits on forgiveness? Yet, in the same way that God's mercy is limitless, our ability to forgive also has to be limitless.

Christ's answer to Peter was that he should not limit himself to forgiving a person only seven times, but rather seventy times seven, or four hundred and ninety times (verse 22). This is not a magic number. Christ was not telling Peter that if, by chance, someone had offended him four hundred and ninety one times that he could then start to refuse forgiveness. Not at all! The Master was teaching that forgiveness has no limit.

Such a commandment is not easy to accept and practise. We are often able to forgive a person once or twice, but if he keeps on offending us, we start doubting the wisdom of forgiveness. We begin to feel as though our "kindness" is being taken advantage of and are tempted to get back at the person in some way or other.

If a person is repentant and sincerely wants to be forgiven, we have to forgive him. This would be impossible if God had left us to struggle on our own. Instead, He has sent His Spirit to live in those who are His faithful servants. If they live by the power of the Spirit, they will recognise the truth of Paul's words to the Philippians: *"For it is God who works in you both to will and to do for His good pleasure."* (Philippians 2:13)

God does not require payment for His forgiveness. Eternal life is a gift from the Creator to all who seek Him (see Romans 6:23).

Now, let us see what attitude the servant in that Biblical passage took immediately after he had been forgiven (Matthew 18:28-30). His immense debt had been forgiven, yet he refused to forgive a friend's small debt. He refused even to give him the opportunity to work off his debt; instead, he threw him in jail.

After reading this parable, we usually exclaim, "What an ungrateful servant!" – without realising that he represents ungrateful Christians. What is the usual response to God's complete forgiveness through Christ? Just like the servant's. God's mercy has freed us from the punishment that our sins deserve, yet we refuse to forgive our brothers in Christ for the harm they have caused us.

God does not simply demand that Christians forgive other people. Rather, He makes it a condition to receiving His forgiveness. This is crystal clear in Matthew 6:14,15. A Christian must be merciful to receive mercy. In addition, our forgiveness has to be sincere; it cannot be mere words. God demands that it come from the heart (Matthew 18:35).

If this seems extremely difficult to do, read the disciples' question and Christ's answer in Matthew 19:25,26. Remember that the God who forgives is also *able to keep you from stumbling, and to present you faultless before the presence of His glory with exceeding joy.* (Jude 1:24)

The spirit of intolerance is not new. It has existed in man since the very beginning and has, time and again, stained the history of the world with death, war and every other kind of evil.

We frequently come in contact with people who appear to be Christian – people who put on a façade of being Christian in order to show off their "faith" to the world. However, they live in misery, in a continual search for words to fill the emptiness they feel. They see other people advancing in the faith and knowledge of the Lord Jesus, but they remain paralysed in their own faith, simply because they do not practise the law of forgiveness. They choose to hold on to bad feelings for others in their hearts, and as a result their faith brings no benefit to their "Christian" life.

BE ANGRY AND DO NOT SIN

It is hard not to be affected by the rotten, corrupt and unjust society we live in. Hardly one day goes by without us committing faults and mistakes. We have to admit that we are at times enwrapped in feelings of anger and indignation at the sight of so much suffering, abuse and injustice. Some theologians refer to this as "righteous anger" – an attitude that every true Christian must have.

"Righteous anger" comes either from God – as in the case of the Lord Jesus: *Then Jesus went into the temple of God and drove out all those who bought and sold in the temple, and overturned the tables of the money changers and the seats of those who sold doves*" (Matthew 21:12) – or from our own human nature.

In either case, righteous anger should never be confused with any other kind of anger, as is common among those who live by their flesh – unbelievers who love themselves more than they love God. They give free reign to anger because of the selfishness of their own hearts. This anger is completely different from the anger that the Bible accepts.

As Christians, we can get angry about injustices committed against the people of God, and even defend the Work of God and His House. But righteous anger never seeks any kind of personal benefit. There are many who say that they are of God, yet these very same people insist on twisting the meaning of the word: *"Be angry, and do not sin: do not let the sun go down on your wrath."* (Ephesians 4:26)

I believe the anger that the Bible talks about is the one we experience in our ministry, whenever we see misery and pain, or when we hear Satan making absurd statements through the mouths of those who are his servants. In such moments, my heart burns with anger against the devil and his demons.

My anger is kindled when I read newspaper articles that speak of politicians creating laws that force children to be taught pagan things in school – things that are totally contrary to the Holy Scriptures. This is precisely the kind of anger that we are allowed to feel. Martin Luther once confessed, "When I am angry, I can write, pray or preach well, because all my temper is stimulated, my understanding is whetted and all worries and worldly temptations gone away."

When anger is not biblical, I mean, when it is selfish, we must be careful not to allow it to lead to bitterness. For this reason, the apostle Paul admonishes us not to let the sun go down on our wrath.

Obviously, he meant that when we feel anger, regardless of the reason, it must immediately be cut off, in order to avoid it bringing harm to us or others. King David also said, *"Be angry, and do not sin. Meditate within your heart on your bed, and be still."* (Psalms 4:4)

Feelings of anger must be short-lived. If not, they will create a stronghold of evil that will be very difficult to demolish even when we are ready to forgive.

A lady once came to my office in the church to ask for help. She had suffered since the day she got married, and things had worsened daily after she had divorced her husband. Diseases, infirmities, financial problems and despair troubled her.

After some months, she had already made some chains of prayer in the church and her life had improved greatly. Her financial situation was much better; the diseases and illnesses were all gone. However, something was still missing. She was not completely happy, as God wants us to be. So I asked her if she was holding onto anything that could have turned into a grudge.

After she admitted to having resentment against her husband, I told her that if she did not expel those feelings from her heart she would never be totally blessed, and would have even more problems in the future. She then asked, "How can I do that if I don't really want to forgive him?" I advised her to ask the Holy Spirit to help her and He would give her the forgiving spirit that she needed.

Thank God, not only did she forgive her husband, but also their marriage was healed after ten years of separation. Now their children have given their lives to God. Today there is joy, peace and abundance in their home because the spirit of forgiveness allowed the Holy Spirit to work in their family.

Submission

Submission is a willingness to yield or surrender to an established authority – to behave humbly before that authority. The Bible is filled with examples of people who were insubordinate and rebellious towards God's established authorities, who wanted positions of authority without the guidance of the Holy Spirit. The consequences were drastic, as we can see in the following cases:

GOD VS. LUCIFER

"I will be like the Most High." (Isaiah 14:14)

Due to greed for God's authority and a readiness to revolt against it, Lucifer (which means "full of light") became Satan – or the devil.

The consequences were terrible in every single aspect. One was that he swept a third of the angels from Heaven and flung them to earth.

"His tail drew a third of the stars of heaven and threw them to the earth." (Revelation 12:4)

Those who follow a rebel become as much a rebel as their leader, and the punishment that their leader receives will be felt by every one of them. The dragon's tail symbolises Satan's rebellion; he took with him one third of the angels, or stars, of

Heaven, presently known as demons. Throughout the years the same thing continues to happen. Those who rebel against God's established authorities are in reality rebelling against God. Therefore, not only they, but all of their followers, have reaped and will reap the fruits of disobedience.

MOSES VS. MIRIAM

Moses was established by God as the authority over the people of Israel, despite the fact that he had initially tried to refuse this leadership. We see Moses' dramatic reluctance before God in Exodus 4. In the middle of the desert, when the people were surrounded by trials and difficulties, one of the biggest rebellions against God's servant took place.

It is interesting to note that rebellion and disobedience always occur at crucial moments when unity and cooperation are vital. Moses was dealing with a big problem: the Jewish people were tired of eating manna; they wanted meat.

There were no animals for food in the desert. So the people began to complain about God and Moses, saying that, although they had been slaves in Egypt, they had had plenty of fish, cucumbers, melons, leeks, onions and garlic to eat; *"but now (...) there is nothing at all except this manna before our eyes!"* (Numbers 11:5,6)

Taking advantage of Moses' embarrassing situation and of his weakness (he had married an Ethiopian woman), Miriam and Aaron tried to incite the people to rebel against the Lord's anointed, saying, *"Has the LORD indeed spoken only through Moses? Has He not spoken through us also?"* (Numbers 12:2)

Insubordination normally begins this way: "He has the Holy Spirit, but so do I. God works through him, but He will do the same through me...I do not need to submit to him, I do not need to obey anyone..." To make matters worse, people who are not spiritually free will give this person "advice" inspired by Satan himself. After the first person has made a comment, someone else will come along, and after him, someone else, until the rebellion and insubordination have had a widespread, negative effect.

"Suddenly the LORD said to Moses, Aaron, and Miriam, 'Come out, you three, to the tabernacle of meeting!' So the three came out. Then the LORD came down in the pillar of cloud and stood in the door of the tabernacle, and called Aaron and Miriam. And they both went forward. Then He said, 'Hear now My words: If there is a prophet among you, I, the LORD, make Myself known to him in a vision; I speak to him in a dream. Not so with My servant Moses; He is faithful in all My house. I speak with him face to face, even plainly, and not in dark sayings; and he sees the form of the LORD. Why then were you not afraid to speak against My servant Moses?' So the anger of the LORD was aroused against them, and He departed."

Numbers 12:4-9

Any move against the delegated authority of God is dangerous, whether or not that authority is being unjust. For example, though I act unjustly towards my daughters, they are still my daughters and I am still their father. I retain the authority as their father. In the same way, when a pastor is unjust to the members of his church, or when he commits sin, he retains the position of "God's anointed", but will be asked to give an account of his behaviour to God.

No one has the right to rise up against God's representative authority. God Himself determines who is removed and who is allowed to stay in a position of spiritual authority. We should never attempt to play God's role and attack the Lord's anointed or slander their spiritual authority.

Look at the example of the people of Israel. Miriam and Aaron's reasoning was sound, but their attitude was all wrong. Their reason for rebelling was that Moses had married an Ethiopian woman. First of all, he already had a wife, and secondly, the Ethiopians were not a part of the people of Israel. So Aaron and Miriam assumed God's role and judged the servant of the Lord.

As a result, Miriam became leprous and, even after Moses prayed for her, she had to remain outside of the camp for seven days. Though she was Moses' sister, she was humiliated for what she had done. It is essential for Christians to live in total and complete submission. If a person is unwilling to submit to those that he can see, how will he ever submit to the Lord Jesus, whom he cannot see?

MOSES VS. KORAH

Korah, Dathan, Abiram and two hundred and fifty leaders of the congregation rose up against Moses and Aaron, saying, *"You take too much upon yourselves, for all the congregation is holy, every one of them, and the LORD is among them. Why then do you exalt yourselves above the assembly of the LORD?"* (Numbers 16:3)

Again, we see Moses having to deal with problems of insubordination among his people and, once more, the consequences were terrible. This time, the number of lives lost was much greater. The second major rebellion followed Miriam's example. She had planted the seed of rebellion in the hearts of many of the people. More than fifteen thousand people, including women and children, who had nothing to do with the matter, died because of one act of rebellion against the servant of the Lord.

Read chapter 16 of the book of Numbers and make your own conclusions. The Bible contains many examples of rebellion and insubordination in order for us to learn from others, and avoid the same mistakes. When the Lord Jesus started teaching His disciples, the very first lesson was about humility: *"Blessed are the poor in spirit, for theirs is the kingdom of heaven."* (Matthew 5:3)

Humility is an attitude of respect, submission and obedience. The Lord Jesus knew that humility – that is, submission – was the first thing to be learned by the disciples. How could the Work of God spread throughout the world if there was no willingness to submit to and obey the authorities that God had established?

So, we conclude by saying, *"through love serve one another."* (Galatians 5:13)

7

Discretion

Discretion is a virtue that must not be forgotten when it comes to a Christian's behaviour before the Lord Jesus Christ. In fact, as long as our horizontal relationships are bad – person to person relationships – our vertical relationship will be bad – communion of man with God in all its fullness. Let me touch briefly on a few but vital points about this subject. They will help you have a life filled with the Lord's blessings.

Noah's nakedness

"And Noah began to be a farmer, and he planted a vineyard. Then he drank of the wine and was drunk, and became uncovered in his tent. And Ham, the father of Canaan, saw the nakedness of his father, and told his two brothers outside. But Shem and Japheth took a garment, laid it on both their shoulders, and went backward and covered the nakedness of their father. Their faces were turned away, and they did not see their father's nakedness. So, Noah awoke from his wine, and knew what his younger son had done to him. Then he said: 'Cursed be Canaan;

a servant of servants he shall be to his brethren.' And he said: 'Blessed be the LORD, the God of Shem, and may Canaan be his servant. May God enlarge Japheth, and may he dwell in the tents of Shem; and may Canaan be his servant.'"

Genesis 9:20-27

The nakedness in this passage symbolises the mistakes and faults of a spiritual leader within a Christian community, or church. The spiritual leader, pastor or person in the position of spiritual authority, has a moral obligation to set the example for his followers, just as our Lord Jesus was an example for His disciples. The spiritual leader of a community must be seen as Jesus Himself, for he is Jesus' representative for his people. Because of this, the community should not be looking for his imperfections and mistakes.

Note that Noah's behaviour was not judged in the story above – not when he got drunk, nor when he was lying uncovered in his tent, nor when he allowed his youngest son to see his nakedness. The whole point of this passage is the youngest son's attitude towards his father's faults. Just as Ham should never have told his brothers that he had seen his father's nakedness, caution and discretion should be practised inside the church. No one should expose publicly either the spiritual leader's mistakes or his own brother's mistakes, even the most intimate ones.

If you find yourself in a situation like Ham's, under no circumstance should you expose it*, because not everyone has the spiritual strength to bear such a burden. All

* Instead of exposing the fault to just anybody, report the matter to one or two authorities in the church who can consider it and apply the necessary steps for correction.

Christians have their own "nakedness" – nobody is perfect. The Holy Spirit living inside of us knows exactly who we are and has seen our nakedness. Yet, in spite of that, He wants to live inside of us. Which one of us, then, should presume that he has the right to expose another person's nakedness?

Ham did not lie to his brothers in this passage. Nevertheless, his sin was considered so serious that his entire generation was cursed. This is a lesson for those who see their brother's nakedness and faults, and then go out and tell everyone they know about it. A lot of people are filled with faith, but are unable to control the impulse of their tongues when certain satanic "opportunities" arise.

This is why many people are in hell, and why many others will soon join them – people who heard about someone's nakedness and revealed it to others who were then destroyed by those words. The apostle James gives us a strong rebuke regarding the sins of the tongue and our duty to control it: *"For we all stumble in many things. If anyone does not stumble in word, he is a perfect man, able also to bridle the whole body (…) the tongue is a little member and boasts great things. See how great a forest a little fire kindles! And the tongue is a fire, a world of iniquity (…) With it we bless our God and Father, and with it we curse men, who have been made in the similitude of God. Out of the same mouth proceed blessing and cursing. My brethren, these things ought not to be so."*

James 3:2-10

Our Lord Jesus said, *"Do you not yet understand that whatever enters the mouth goes into the stomach and is eliminated?*

But those things which proceed out of the mouth come from the heart, and they defile a man." (Matthew 15:17,18)

If God considers the human tongue to be a fire and a world of iniquity, surely we must watch our words in order to avoid sending the "Harvest of the Lord" into the flames of hell. Instead of adding more fuel to the fire, each one of us, as true Christians, should extinguish the fire of destructive words with the "water of life" that dwells inside of us.

As it is written, *"He who covers a transgression seeks love, but he who repeats a matter separates friends."* (Proverbs 17:9)

When the Bible recommends discretion towards the sins of other people, its goal is to protect the many souls that have already been redeemed by the blood of our Lord. We have seen many abandon their Christian faith simply because they heard about faults and sins of brothers and pastors who, in a moment of weakness, committed serious mistakes. And yet our decision not to publicise these mistakes does not mean that we condone them. On the contrary, it is because we do not approve of them that we want to bury them.

Noah's nakedness has always existed and will continue to exist as long as man lives in the flesh. It is the legacy of sin left by Adam, the first to experience nakedness as sin.

"I heard Your voice in the garden, and I was afraid because I was naked; and I hid myself." (Genesis 3:10)

As a result, the Lord clothed Adam and his wife in animal skins. Today the blood of God's Lamb, Jesus Christ, covers our nakedness! Hallelujah. And that is why we no longer need to fear or hide from God. Our only concern is about someone else exposing our nakedness and making us into an object of shame.

The only person truly interested in shaming us before God and the world is Satan himself. We have to join forces and cover each other's faults, especially those of our brothers in faith, so that the devil will be deprived of winning a victory over the followers of the Lord Jesus Christ. When a serious mistake of a brother or pastor of a certain Christian community is publicised, that community is devastated, just as the Lord Jesus said: *"Every kingdom divided against itself is brought to desolation, and every city or house divided against itself will not stand."* (Matthew 12:25)

If a brother or pastor commits a serious sin, and people hear about it, that brother or pastor will be met with understanding, love and even compassion from some people. Others, however, will respond with repulsion and disgust, and so, the division starts and the community is ultimately destroyed. But if the brother or pastor's weaknesses are covered over, then the Holy Spirit will be free to work. God will not allow His son's nakedness to be a stumbling block for those who worship Him, and so He will speak to his heart through His Word in such an efficient manner that it will be unnecessary to ask for anyone's help.

I believe we can compare the dangerous attitude of Christians revealing each other's sins to a football game. The Lord's followers are on one team playing against Satan and his team. After many attempts at a goal, suddenly, a Christian scores a goal – but for the other team! When this happens the Christians have to double their efforts in order to win. The devil, at times, triumphs over Christians because they have become a divided team, each doing what he wants, while at the same time our beloved Shepherd is losing great numbers of sheep to the enemy.

My dear brother, let us be extremely careful about the things we say.

"For we all stumble in many things. If anyone does not stumble in word, he is a perfect man, able also to bridle the whole body." (James 3:2)

Let us use our mouth to bring shame to Satan, our enemy, to glorify the name of our Lord Jesus Christ, and to proclaim the Gospel of Peace throughout the world, in the name of our Lord Almighty.

Fasting

Fasting is a partial or total abstinence from food. Its purpose is to deny the physical body in order to gain more spiritual strength. We are not saying that our physical body needs to be punished. What we are saying is that when a person fasts, his spirit is freed and as a consequence he is enabled to seek out God, who is Spirit, in a deep and personal way.

During a fast a person's spirit feels more and more confident as the desires of his flesh are made void by the strength of his spirit. We consider fasting a more devoted prayer than one made with the lips because it involves inexpressible cries of a person's soul in search of the blessings of God.

A partial fast is when a person abstains from food alone, like Jesus did during his forty days in the desert. He ate nothing at all (Luke 4:2). The Bible does not make any reference to water, but we imagine that He must have drunk water; otherwise, the gospels would have mentioned it. This is a partial fast – when a person stops eating food but does not stop drinking water. A fast is also considered partial when a person stops eating and drinking food and water, but maintains sexual relations with his or her wife or husband. A fast is partial whenever the needs of the flesh are satisfied in any way and at a minimum level.

A total fast is when a person abstains from everything pertaining to his physical body. For instance, when Moses *"was there with the LORD forty days and forty nights; he neither ate bread nor drank water. And He wrote on the tablets the words of the covenant, the Ten Commandments."* (Exodus 34:28)

The flesh is completely denied and the spirit given total freedom in a total fast. In a partial fast freedom is given to the spirit, however only partially. And yet, we should not say that one fast is more important than another because in the end both are true fasts. The value of a fast depends on the person, his faith, and the longings for God in his heart.

In our opinion, both are effective as long as they are made with a real desire for God's will to be done. If your body is not strong enough to withstand a total fast, we suggest the partial fast. But if you are healthy and strong and have the desire in your heart, then you should make a total fast.

Unless you approach fasting in a spirit of prayer and humility before God, it will be useless. How can fasting be effective if a person treats it lightly, as if it were a joke? When a person on a fast looks for something to distract himself, say, like entertainment, it is a sign that his fast is nothing but a meaningless observance. Many people make total fasts at intervals all through their lives without seeing any real spiritual benefit because they make them with resentment in their hearts, to show off to the world. On the contrary, true fasting, either partial or total, is made with the purpose of drawing close to God, and so material things are ignored as much as possible.

WHEN TO FAST

A fast should not begin immediately after any meal, but at least three hours after the last meal. If a person wants to fast for six hours, he should start his fast three hours after his last meal. In other words, to make a six-hour fast you will have to abstain from food for nine hours after your last meal.

Fasts should be made for these types of situations:

▶ In times of tragedy (2 Samuel 1:12)

▶ When the Church is experiencing hardships (Luke 5:33-35)

▶ When friends or acquaintances are being attacked (Psalms 35:13)

▶ In personal affliction (2 Samuel 12:16)

▶ In times of danger (Esther 4:16)

▶ When the Lord's ministers are being consecrated (Acts 13:3, 14:23)

Tithes and offerings

It is the Holy Spirit who directs His Church and, through its members, He establishes the Kingdom of God on earth. However, the Church of the Lord Jesus Christ would never be able to spread the message of salvation to all nations without money. For this reason, God determined that tithes and offerings should be given in the church, and that they would be used to spread the Word of Jesus Christ, the Saviour.

The Holy Spirit has made us understand that money is to the Church what blood is to the human body. It enables us to use various means of communication to reach people who are at home, in hospitals and in prisons and tell them about eternal life. Billions of people are going to spend eternity in hell simply because no one ever spoke to them about salvation in Christ Jesus. And if no one ever spoke to them about Christ, this can only mean that too few people funded missionary efforts with their tithes and offerings.

If Christians all over the world were more passionate about lost souls, they would not hesitate to sponsor the Work of God, and the power of mass communication would not be in the hands of so many unbelievers.

Imagine if you who know the Bible and have a strong desire to save souls had the opportunity to speak on radio or TV and were able to broadcast it worldwide. How many souls would you win for the Lord Jesus? Unfortunately, this is not possible because there is not enough money to pay for such broadcasts. It is a sad thing to say, but this reveals that not every Christian is doing his best; otherwise, everything would be possible. The apostle Paul said, *"I can do all things through Christ who strengthens me."* (Philippians 4:13)

Money is essential in the Work of God. It can transform the world by making the widespread preaching of the living and powerful Gospel of the Lord Jesus Christ a reality. Money is so important to the Work of God that God Himself allows us to test Him with it (Malachi 3:10).

Everyone should desire to be financially blessed and to enjoy God's great generosity, thereby verifying that God is truly the owner of all the gold and silver on earth, as it is written, *'The silver is Mine, and the gold is Mine', says the* LORD *of hosts."* (Haggai 2:8)

When we pay our tithes to God, He is bound by His own promise to fulfil His Word and rebuke the devouring spirits that destroy people's lives by causing illnesses, accidents, addictions, misery and other similar things.

When we are faithful tithers, we are protected from these attacks and are able to enjoy the abundance of life on earth, because God is by our side, blessing us in everything we do. According to the Bible, the tithe is not only a tenth of our income; it is the first fruit and must be dedicated to God.

As citizens, we pay taxes to the government, which are used for the benefit of the nation. Likewise, the Lord implemented the tithe so that the Church would be able to reach out to and help those who are in darkness.

"IMPORTANT THINGS"

The tithe is important for God and for the Church. In a capitalist society it is impossible for the Church to save the lost without money.

Giving tithes has great impact on the life of a tither. Abraham, for example, could only be blessed after paying his tithe to Melchizedek. Only after this act of faith, submission and loyalty, did God establish His covenant with him, saying, *"Do not be afraid, Abram. I am your shield, your exceedingly great reward."* (Genesis 15:1)

Abraham became the father of the great nation of Israel and, ultimately, an ancestor of Jesus, our Saviour.

The tithe is so important that it was implemented long before the Ten Commandments came into being. If it was important both before and during the period of the Law, why would it not be important now, after the Law?

On a certain occasion, Jesus was rebuking the scribes and Pharisees for being so stiff-necked concerning their practice of the Law. He taught them that justice, mercy and faith were the most important things to be learned from the Law of Moses, but that they should not ignore the other commandments, which were equally important. One of the important things that Jesus referred to was the tithe.

"Woe to you, scribes and Pharisees, hypocrites! For you pay tithe of mint and anise and cummin, and have neglected the weightier matters of the law: justice and mercy and faith. These you ought to have done, without leaving the others undone."

Matthew 23:23

When we speak about the tithe, we are often ridiculed, criticised and opposed by unbelievers. Obviously, when a person lacks spiritual discernment, he may understand the meaning of the tithe, but he will find it extremely difficult to actually keep this commandment.

Those who do not understand God on this subject, or who actually disagree with Him, will obviously find it impossible to give 10% of their income to the Church when they are not sure what will be done with it. Their money is normally the result of hard work and sweat. Nevertheless, millions of people have been blessed by dedicating the tenth part of what they earn to the Lord.

AN OWNER'S RIGHTS

The following example may shed some light on this subject. When a person has an uncultivated piece of farmland, he makes an agreement and rents it out. The farmer clears the land, ploughs it, rids the land of harmful pests and insects, and finally sows his seed and cares for the land until the harvest. After the harvest, he pays the landlord the percentage of his harvest previously agreed upon, usually 50%.

The landlord does nothing but wait for the guaranteed income. So when God demands 10% of our income, He is in fact demanding little compared to all that He has given to us.

Our life, our intelligence, our energy, the land, the rain, the sun and everything else on earth and in heaven belong to Him, and we are nothing but mere overseers.

THE RIGHT TO CHALLENGE

Who has the right to put God to the test, challenging Him to do the things He has promised? A tither! God Himself invites us to put Him to the test – one of the main reasons why we should tithe. He says,

"'Bring all the tithes into the storehouse, that there may be food in My house, and try Me now in this,' says the LORD of hosts, 'If I will not open for you the windows of heaven and pour out for you such blessing that there will not be room enough to receive it.'"

Malachi 3:10

Many famous people have tested God with their tithe and become millionaires: the founders of Colgate and Caterpillar, as well as Henry Ford. Those who follow their example and devote as much attention to being faithful to God as to accumulating wealth and building businesses will start to be more and more blessed each and every day.

I invite you who are reading this book at this very moment to become a tither and experience not only the love of God, but His plan for your finances. Test God in this way and then stand back and see what He will do to your life. Everyone will be amazed at your prosperity. You will never run out of money. On the contrary, you will have plenty and will be able to buy things you have always wanted to buy but have never been able to. You will never lack a thing, because the Lord will be with you.

"The LORD is my shepherd; I shall not want." (Psalms 23:1)

Peace, joy, happiness and pleasure; an abundance of food, energy and strength; health, love and life – all these things are waiting for you, but for them to be yours you have to practise this simple, but very important thing.

One of the greatest revelations in life is that God wants to be man's partner. When man cooperates with God, he will have the opportunity to take part in God's blessings and will spread His Word.

God created man in His image and likeness so that the created and the Creator could enjoy a close relationship. Just as He made covenants with Adam, Moses, Abraham, Isaac and Jacob, He wants to make covenants with us.

The basis of this covenant with God is: Whatever belongs to us (life, strength, money) is given to God; and whatever belongs to Him (blessings, peace, happiness, joy) is given to us. We become partners with God. The Bible says we are co-heirs of Christ and heirs of God.

"Therefore you are no longer a slave but a son, and if a son, then an heir of God through Christ." (Galatians 4:7)

One of the things that amazes me the most is God's concern for people. Throughout the Bible God invites people to have communion with Him so that they can find happiness.

God blesses all who seek Him in spirit and in truth. When we become God's partners, we are committed to each other. He gives us abundant life and daily communion with Him, just as He did with Adam and Eve before their disobedience.

The blessings that come through tithing are unlimited. A faithful tither is continually blessed in his finances and in all that he does physically and spiritually. The tithe blesses all areas of a person's life because it is, and has always been, a part of God's creation.

When God created the earth and everything on it, He took one day to rest, which represents the tithe. When God handed the Garden of Eden over to Adam and Eve, He gave them everything in it, except for the tree of the knowledge of good and evil. It also represented the tithe.

The Lord Jesus Himself is a kind of tithe. God gave Him so that we could take part in His divine nature. Therefore, the tithe is essential for the financial, spiritual and physical areas of a Christian's life.

THE DIFFERENCE BETWEEN TITHES AND OFFERINGS

As water is different from wine, tithes are different from offerings.

The tithe is the first 10% of all the money we receive, whether it is wages, the sale of a property or car, or a gift. According to the Bible, all people are to give 10% of everything they receive.

Offerings are the opposite of tithes. A person gives when and what he wants, nothing is compulsory.

Blessings that come through offerings

Offerings bring many blessings, but not as many as the tithe, (in the case of the tithe they are limitless). Blessings that come as a result of offerings are relative. For example, when Abel and Cain presented their offerings to the Lord, Abel brought the firstborn, that is, the first fruits of his flock; and Cain brought some of the fruits of the soil. The Bible says that God honoured Abel and his offering but He did not honour Cain and his offering. This is because Abel's offering had been carefully chosen, and Cain's had not. Cain did not present the first fruits to God.

In the same way, the Lord praised the poor widow when she gave everything she had: two insignificant coins.

When a person brings an offering to God, He is not concerned about the amount that a person is giving, but whether it is the best that that person can bring. God never looks at what a person brings in his hands, but rather, at what is left in his pocket.

The value of an offering is measured by the amount that a person could have given. Jesus said that the poor widow gave much more than the rich men, who had given large sums of money. Why is that? Because she gave everything she had. The rich men gave a lot of money, but it was the excess of what they had in their pockets, like table scraps thrown to pigs. They regarded God as a fool.

Offerings are blessed when they are given out of love and dedication. We receive according to what we give. If you sow little, you will reap little. Offerings are so important that the apostle Paul dedicated two chapters of his second epistle to the Corinthians to this subject (2 Corinthians 8 and 9).

When we bring our tithes, God sees that we are faithful to Him. When we bring our offerings, He sees that we love Him and are dedicated to His Work. In both situations, God gives us the opportunity to prove to Him how much we really love Him. He said, *"For where your treasure is, there your heart will be also."* (Luke 12:34)

Money is as important to the Work of God as blood is to the human body. At times God allows His people to go through financial hardships so that the church leader will feel compelled to teach them to give offerings and tithes. Jesus said, *"Give and it will be given to you: good measure, pressed down, shaken together, and running over will be put into your bosom. For with the same measure that you use, it will be measured back to you."* (Luke 6:38)

For a person to receive a good measure, pressed down, shaken together and running over, he has to first learn to give. As he gives, he receives. The apostle Paul instructed Timothy, saying, *"For the love of money is a root of all kinds of evil, for which some have strayed from the faith in their greediness, and pierced themselves through with many sorrows."* (1 Timothy 6:10)

Money itself is not the root of all kinds of evil. The love of money is what enslaves people. God asks His children to give tithes and offerings as a way of testing the nature of their love.

The origin of the Lord's Supper

"*Now on the first day of the Feast of Unleavened Bread the disciples came to Jesus, saying to Him, 'Where do You want us to prepare for You to eat the Passover?' And He said, 'Go into the city to a certain man, and say to Him, "The Teacher says, 'My time is at hand; I will keep the Passover at your house with My disciples. So the disciples did as Jesus had directed them and they prepared the Passover.*"

Matthew 26:17-19

This passage clearly shows that the disciples did not yet know anything about the Lord's Supper. They were expecting to celebrate the Passover, the Feast of Unleavened Bread, which was one of the most important religious festivals in the Jewish calendar. It was a celebration of the day that Israel was delivered from its Egyptian slavery, a feast day established just before God sent the tenth and last plague upon the land of Egypt.

The Lord commanded each family to choose a lamb without defect for sacrifice. They were then to take some of the lamb's blood and smear it on the top of the door-frame of the house where the roasted lamb would be eaten, along with bitter herbs and bread made without yeast. The participants were to wear their travelling clothes as they ate the meal, as though prepared for a long journey, with sandals on their feet and a walking stick in their hands (Exodus 12).

In fact, the entire Passover ceremony indirectly pointed to the Saviour.

"And as they were eating, Jesus took bread, blessed and broke it, and gave it to the disciples and said, 'Take, eat; this is My body.' Then He took the cup, and gave it to them, saying, 'Drink from it, all of you. For this is My blood of the new covenant, which is shed for many for the remission of sins.'

Matthew 26:26-28

The Lord Jesus had taken part in the Passover before establishing the Lord's Supper. Although He did not openly associate the two, we can clearly understand that He wanted to establish a feast for those who would accept Him as Saviour. This new feast would be parallel to the Passover and have the same spiritual significance.

As the Jewish people celebrated the Passover in remembrance of the day they were delivered, the Gentiles who accepted the Lord Jesus as their Saviour would celebrate the Lord's Supper in remembrance of the day they were cleansed from their sins and delivered from hell. That is why the Lord Jesus established the Lord's Supper.

The Lord's Supper symbolises communion with the Lord Jesus. It is written, *"The cup of blessing which we bless, is it not the communion of the blood of Christ? The bread which we break, is it not the communion of the body of Christ?"* (1 Corinthians 10:16)

Since we all partake of the same bread there should be unity in the Church; we are one bread and we all have the nature of the Lord Jesus Christ, as it is written in 1 Corinthians 10:17: *"For we, though many, are one bread and one body; for we all partake of that one bread."*

Through the apostle Paul's words, we see the spirit that permeated the hearts of those who participated in the Lord's Supper.

As the first Christians were Jews, the Passover was incorporated into the Lord's Supper. It became a common practice for participants to take part in the Passover meal before the Lord's Supper, as the Lord Jesus Himself had done. But during the meal some would eat and drink to such an extent that they would end up drunk, as happened in the church of Corinth. For this reason, the apostle Paul warned them severely, as described in 1 Corinthians 11:17-22:

"Now, in giving these instructions I do not praise you, since you come together not for the better but for the worse. For first of all, when you come together as a church, I hear that there are divisions among you, and in part I believe it. For there must also be factions among you, that those who are approved may be recognised among you. Therefore when you come together in

one place, it is not to eat the Lord's Supper. For in eating, each one takes his own supper ahead of others; and one is hungry and another is drunk. What! Do you not have houses to eat and drink in? Or do you despise the church of God and shame those who have nothing? What shall I say to you? Shall I praise you in this? I do not praise you."

The Lord's Supper in the church of Corinth was sharply criticised by Paul because it was not celebrated in the Spirit of Christ, but in the flesh. From that moment on, the apostle Paul put an end to the meal that was eaten before the Lord's Supper.

The Lord's Supper is a true feast for our physical and spiritual bodies.

THE MEANING OF THE LORD'S SUPPER

When the Lord Jesus declared that the bread He had just consecrated, broken and given to His disciples was His body, He was in fact revealing the true meaning of His physical life. The bread represents His strength and health, which is given on behalf of all who accept Him as Saviour, so that they can enjoy both His nature and His physical health. That is why the prophet Isaiah affirmed, *"Surely He has borne our griefs and carried our sorrows..."* (Isaiah 53:4)

His flesh bore all disease and infirmity; therefore, we should not accept illnesses. Satan no longer has the right to rule over our physical bodies because, by faith, they are in communion with the Lord Jesus through the Lord's Supper. Jesus said, *"...this is My body."* (Mark 14:22)

Likewise, Jesus blessed the wine and gave it to the disciples, saying, *"For this is My blood of the new covenant, which is shed for many for the remission of sins."* (Matthew 26:28)

Flesh and blood are interdependent; therefore, both the bread and the wine are important. They point to the fact that those who believe in the Lord Jesus have the right to eternal life.

This new and latest covenant places Christians squarely before God, the Father. They become genuine children, who have obligations and enjoy privileges. Among these privileges is the power to communicate with God in the same way that the Lord Jesus did, and to be baptised in the Holy Spirit.

The covenant that the Lord Jesus spoke about can be compared to the covenant on a wedding day, when both bride and groom leave behind their own way of living. When a man enters into a marriage covenant with a woman, he is saying that from that moment on he will live for her; that his desire will be to meet her needs; that he will be faithful to her until death, etc. The woman, in turn, leaves her parents' house and is joined to her husband; she submits to him and him alone; she cares for him more than she cares for herself, etc. At least, this is what should happen, according to the Bible. A covenant with the Lord Jesus through His blood demands the same, or higher, level of commitment from each of the parties involved.

Bearing these things in mind, we should prepare our hearts whenever we take part in the Lord's Supper. We should expect to enjoy an abundance of joy and happiness in the Holy Spirit for all that it represents.

The Lord's Supper announces our Lord's glorious ministry: the healings and extraordinary miracles He performed;

His compassion and care for the poor and oppressed; His great and magnificent victory over the devil and his demons; and His death and resurrection on the third day.

To summarise, in the same way that the body of the Lord Jesus (the bread) gives us physical health, his blood (the wine) gives us spiritual health.

WHO CAN TAKE PART IN THE LORD'S SUPPER?

The apostle Paul gave the following instructions:

"Therefore whoever eats this bread or drinks this cup of the Lord in an unworthy manner will be guilty of the body and blood of the Lord. But let a man examine himself, and so let him eat of the bread and drink of the cup. For he who eats and drinks in an unworthy manner eats and drinks judgement to himself, not discerning the Lord's body. For this reason many are weak and sick among you, and may sleep."

1 Corinthians 11:27-30

The apostle did not go into detail about what he meant by an unworthy manner. However, we gather that only those whose lives have been washed in the blood of the Lamb can eat and drink at the Lord's table; that is, those who have had their consciences purified by the peace of God. As a matter of fact, the apostle Paul, inspired by the Holy Spirit said, *"And let the peace of God rule in your hearts…"* (Colossians 3:15)

The Holy Spirit Himself convicts those who practise this teaching of the fact that they are worthy to take part in the Supper of the Lamb. Those who are unworthy immediately feel accused by a guilty and sinful conscience.

For this reason it is vital for a person to examine himself before taking part in the Lord's Supper. We have to be sure that we are living pure lives before God and that there is nothing to fear from His Spirit, who scrutinises our minds and knows our thoughts. If there is no guilt and a person is absolutely sure that all his sins have been forgiven, then he can, and should, take part in the Lord's Supper, and the Lord Jesus will strengthen him spiritually.

If a person who is converted to the Lord Jesus makes a mistake that brings feelings of guilt, he should confess it to God and ask for forgiveness as soon as possible, as it is written, *"If we confess our sins, He is faithful and just to forgive us our sins and to cleanse us from all unrighteousness."* (1 John 1:9)

It is important to emphasise that it is you who make the decision to participate in the Lord's Supper or not. No other person can make this decision for you.

If you are not sure whether or not to participate in the Lord's Supper, allow the bread and wine to pass you by and wait for a future opportunity. It is better not to participate, than to participate with doubt in your heart. It is also written, *"But he who doubts is condemned if he eats, because he does not eat from faith; for whatever is not from faith is sin."* (Romans 14:23)

Those who take part in the Lord's Supper in an unworthy manner are cursed, because they are eating and drinking judgement on themselves. They will be guilty of sinning against the body and blood of the Lord. That is why many so-called Christians are spiritually weak. They disobey the Word of God and take part in the Lord's Supper in an unworthy manner.

Many are sick and dying for having disregarded the body and the blood of the Lord. This is why so many people have known the Lord Jesus exactly as the Bible describes Him, for many years, but are still spiritually weak and stand as terrible testimonies of the Lord.

The Lord's Supper is not the kind of ceremony that can be celebrated in a frivolous way. Rather, it is a solemn ceremony that demands from its participants a heart full of joy and happiness for the high privilege of sitting at the Lord's table, eating His body and drinking His blood, all in remembrance of His life, death and resurrection.

Baptism in water

Baptism in water is a turning point for those who truly want to start a new life with the Lord Jesus. After His resurrection, the Lord Jesus taught the disciples about its importance by giving them a clear command: "*Go into all the world and preach the gospel to every creature. He who believes and is baptized will be saved; but he who does not believe will be condemned.*" (Mark 16:15,16)

Matthew 28:19 also says, "*Go therefore and make disciples of all the nations, baptizing them in the name of the Father and of the Son and of the Holy Spirit.*"

THE MEANING OF BAPTISM IN WATER

In the same way that a burial ceremony signifies that the last tie between a man and his earthly life has been severed, baptism in water is a public declaration that a believer is severing all ties to his natural life. Our inner self is put to death, and sin no longer has dominion over us.

For this reason, when a person accepts the Lord Jesus as his Saviour and is baptised in water, he abandons a life of sin for a life of doing the will of God. No matter how bad a person's temper, after conversion and baptism in water, he becomes gentle and humble, demonstrating to all around that a true servant of the Lord does not live according to the dictates of this world.

If a person accepts the Lord as his personal Saviour and is baptised and then refuses to abandon his sins, it will only be a matter of time until he leaves Him.

Baptism is the beginning of a new way of life. Through immersion in water – the most natural and purifying element in nature – a person is cleansed from his sins.

When the Israelites left Egypt, it was necessary for them to go through a symbolic baptism in order to live a new life. Their baptism took place in the Red Sea. Noah too was baptised in the water of the Flood so that he could become the patriarch of a new generation on earth.

Before a person can live in newness of life, it is imperative that he be baptised in water. When Philip went down to a city in Samaria and preached Christ to the people there, they all paid close attention to what he said and were baptised in water, both men and women (Acts 8:4-12).

Preparing for baptism in water

A person is ready to be baptised when he is repentant and sure of his faith in the Lord Jesus. This is why we do not baptise children, for baptism requires that a person repent of his sins. How can children repent of sins they have not committed? Instead, children should be dedicated to God, as it is written: *"And He took them up in His arms, laid His hands on them, and blessed them."* (Mark 10:16)

When Peter preached about the Kingdom of God and the Lord Jesus for the first time in Jerusalem, those who were listening were cut to the heart and asked Peter and the other apostles what they should do. Peter replied, *"Repent and be baptized, every one of you, in the name of the Jesus Christ for the forgiveness of your sins. And you will receive the gift of the Holy Spirit."* (Acts 2:38)

Repentance is the basic requirement for a successful baptism in water. And yet, there are many who are baptised without first repenting of their old life. They are convinced of their sins but have not yet been converted to the Lord Jesus. As a result they continually cause problems in the Church: they argue, they fight, they badmouth the pastor and other church servants, etc. In short, they are never happy; they are like fish out of water. They still live under the dominion of sin because their flesh was never buried with Christ.

REPENTANCE

Repentance is a profound feeling of sorrow or regret for wrongs that have been done. It involves the following:

◗ A sinner has to acknowledge his sin. This is the first and most important step to sincere repentance. No one can repent of what he has not acknowledged.

◗ A sinner has to hate sin. If a person does not hate sin, he will, without a doubt, sin again and eventually get to the point that he becomes used to it.

◗ A sinner has to abandon his sin. If a person does not immediately turn his back on sin, he will never be able to leave it. For example, when a person accepts invitations to spend time with people who do not share his faith, he will often give in to their attempts to persuade him to do what is wrong.

▶ A sinner has to completely forget his sin, treating it as though it had never happened.

BAPTISM BY IMMERSION IN WATER – Much has been said about the actual manner of baptism. Many believe that baptism is sprinkling water on a person's head; others believe that baptism is immersion in water but only in the name of Jesus.

We at the UCKG seek to follow the Holy Bible as much as possible. For us baptism is immersion in water, in the name of the Father, of the Son and of the Holy Spirit, as the Lord Jesus Himself commanded in Matthew 28:19.

BAPTISM OF THE SICK

It is quite common for people to accept the Lord Jesus when they are critically ill or close to death. In either case, it is not always feasible to immerse a person in water. The thief on the cross next to the Lord Jesus is a perfect example of this. He knew he was going to die, and recognising that Jesus was indeed the Son of God, he asked for his soul to be saved. Immediately, the Lord Jesus said to him, *"Assuredly, I say to you, today, you will be with Me in Paradise."* (Luke 23:43) And so we see that the thief was saved despite the fact that he had not been baptised in water.

Essentially, baptism in water is meant for those who will go on living in this sinful world after their conversion.

In order to avoid contamination they have to 'kill' their flesh, so that sin will no longer have control over it.

After reading this brief explanation about baptism in water, you should examine your own life. Regardless of any previous baptism, healing or financial blessing, you need to ask yourself if your attitudes and behaviour in the presence of your family and friends have changed by any degree. If you see that there has been no change, you need to repent of your sins and be baptised again – this time for real. With this new baptism you will have the assurance that you are starting a new and perfect life in Jesus Christ.

The Holy Spirit

Before we speak about the baptism in the Holy Spirit, we first need to know about the Holy Spirit Himself.

The work of the Holy Spirit remained largely unknown over the centuries, after His wonderful manifestation in the Primitive Church. But thanks to the Pentecostal movement, which started in the early 1900s, the nations of the world are again able to know more about the Holy Spirit. Pentecostalism is today the fastest growing branch of Christianity.

As the third Person of the Holy Trinity, the Holy Spirit is no less important than the other two Persons. In fact, the Father, the Son (Jesus Christ) and the Holy Spirit are virtually one and the same. They are distinct, yet form only one God. It is an unsolvable mystery. It is as though we are saying, $1+1+1=1$.

The Holy Spirit is also referred to as:

⟩ The Good Spirit (Psalms 143:10)

⟩ The Helper (John 14:16)

- The Spirit (Ephesians 5:18)

- The Holy One (1 John 2:20)

- The Spirit of Adoption (Romans 8:15)

- The Spirit of Love (2 Timothy 1:7)

- The Spirit of Knowledge (Isaiah 11:2)

- The Spirit of Counsel (Isaiah 11:2)

- The Spirit of Christ (Romans 8:9)

- The Spirit of God (Genesis 1:2)

- The Spirit of Understanding, the Spirit of Might, the Spirit of Wisdom, the Spirit of the Lord, the Spirit of the Fear of the Lord (Isaiah 11:2)

- The Spirit of Truth (John 14:17)

He is also symbolised by:

- Water (John 7:38)

- Fire (Psalms 78:14)

- Oil (Psalms 23:5)

- A dove (Matthew 3:16)

- A seal (John 6:27)

- The wind (Acts 2:2)

Since He is the Author of life (John 3:5-8), the Holy Spirit has huge influence on human beings. He is the One who:

- Opens the windows of heaven to us (Matthew 3:16)

- Helps us (John 14:16,17)

- Convicts the world of sin (John 16:8)
- Gives us access to the Father (Ephesians 2:18)
- Causes us to bear fruit (Galatians 5:22,23)
- Gives us boldness to speak about Jesus (Acts 4:31)
- Gives life to our mortal bodies (Romans 8:11)
- Pours out in our hearts the love of God (Romans 5:5)
- Teaches us all things (John 14:26)
- Flows out of our hearts (John 7:38,39)
- Uses us to cast out unclean spirits (Matthew 12:28)
- Guides us (Acts 8:29)
- Inspires us (2 Timothy 3:16)
- Intercedes for us (Romans 8:26)
- Dwells in us (John 14:17)
- Justifies us (1 Corinthians 6:11)
- Reveals the will of God for our lives (Ephesians 3:5)
- Sanctifies us (1 Peter 1:2)
- Bears witness with our spirit that we are children of God (Romans 8:16)

The Holy Spirit is Omnipotent, Omnipresent and Omniscient; as a result, He is able to fill us with happiness and peace, dwell in us, enjoy a close relationship with His people, and perform miracles.

THE HOLY SPIRIT, GOD'S GREATEST GIFT!

The Holy Spirit is the Lord Jesus Christ's greatest gift to His followers.

God could have sent an angel to do the work of the Holy Spirit in our lives, and yet, for reasons beyond our understanding, He chose to give Himself. As a result, our desire is to see every follower of the Lord Jesus to be baptised in the Holy Spirit.

I usually say that those who are baptised with the Spirit are more privileged than the 12 disciples of the Lord Jesus. Every time Jesus left to pray or rest by Himself, they felt alone and were overwhelmed with fear (Mark 4:38). However, once a person is sealed with the Holy Spirit, he is never alone, as it is written: *"And I will pray the Father, and He will give you another Helper, that He may abide with you forever – the Spirit of truth, whom the world cannot receive, because it neither sees Him nor knows Him; but you know Him, for He dwells with you and will be in you."* (John 14:16,17)

The baptism in the Holy Spirit makes us different in every aspect because we take on Jesus' own nature. It makes us see as He saw, think as He thought and speak as He spoke – to act in the same way that Jesus acted. It is this baptism that enables us to do the Work of God. It is written, *"But you shall receive power when the Holy Spirit has come upon you; and you shall be witnesses to Me in Jerusalem, and in all Judea and Samaria, and to the end of the earth."* (Acts 1:8)

We conclude that no one should get directly involved in the Work of God without having received this power. It is quite dangerous for a new convert to try and do anything without the seal of the Holy Spirit because we do not wrestle against flesh and blood, but against spiritual hosts of wickedness (Ephesians 6:12).

If we are going to fight against spiritual forces, we have to put on spiritual armour in order to achieve victory, and nothing is more powerful than the baptism in the Holy Spirit.

The Son of God Himself needed this baptism to perform His earthly ministry; the apostles received it and were able to continue the Lord's ministry; for the same reason, the apostle Paul received this baptism after Ananias laid hands on him (Acts 9:17); and for these and many other reasons, we also need to receive this seal of God in our lives.

Knowing about the Holy Spirit is vital to our faith. Contrary to what many people think, He is not some vague kind of energy or guiding light; rather, He is a spiritual being, with qualities, virtues and a personality. He is a person just like the Lord Jesus Christ and the Father. He has many responsibilities, the most important of which is to lead us to the Lord Jesus.

His greatest desire is to lead us and fill us with His presence, so that we are one with Him. Everything that the Lord Jesus did was the result of the anointing He had received from the Holy Spirit, and now the same Spirit wants to dwell in us.

The Holy Spirit is the greatest gift of the Lord Jesus to His followers. Jesus Himself received the Holy Spirit when He was baptised by John the Baptist; the apostles, the women who followed Jesus and each of the 120 people who were in the custom of assembling together in the temple received the Holy Spirit; three thousand more people who heard Peter's preaching on the day of Pentecost also received the promise. They were baptised in the Holy Spirit because they needed Him. If they needed this blessing, so do we.

The baptism in the Holy Spirit is a unique experience. For a person to receive it, he has to let go of himself, his religious traditions and anything else that interferes in his relationship with God. There must be a strong and sincere desire to receive the Holy Spirit.

Anyone seeking the baptism in the Holy Spirit has to clearly understand God's plan in order for this promise to be fulfilled. The Holy Spirit was sent as a substitute for the Lord Jesus Christ; therefore, if a person wants the baptism in the Holy Spirit and is not ready to follow the Lord Jesus, his efforts are in vain.

Baptism in the Holy Spirit

The baptism in the Holy Spirit is a term used to describe the fullness of God dwelling within a person. However, for this to occur there are some steps to be followed.

▶ No one pours clean water into a dirty cup. Likewise, a person cannot be given the Holy Spirit when there are other spirits dwelling in his body, such as the spirit of envy, dissension, anger, greed, gossip, etc.

▶ No one is given the Spirit of God as long as he holds a grudge against someone else. God's greater forgiveness can only be enjoyed after the person has sincerely forgiven those who hurt him. Only then will the Holy Spirit find a place to dwell in his heart.

▶ No liar is given the Spirit of Truth. Our yes must be 'yes' and our no, 'no'. We have to tell the truth, because it is our sincerity that keeps us clean.

▶ No one can be given the Holy Spirit while he is still attached to the things of this world.

▶ When you seek the baptism in the Holy Spirit you must not let anything accuse you before God. If there is something accusing you, you have to immediately confess it to the Lord Jesus and ask for His forgiveness.

◗ You should not think about your family, your bills, yourself or anything else when seeking the Holy Spirit. Rather than making a silent prayer in your mind, you should worship the Lord Jesus with your mouth, telling Him that you love Him, that He is the most important Person in your life and that you are ready to do His holy will. Don't stop your worship to ask for anything else, like healing or deliverance; force yourself to continue praising Him, and remember to do it audibly with your lips.

◗ If you feel something attempting to distract you, know that you are about to receive the baptism in the Holy Spirit. Obviously the devil will do everything he can to divert your attention and to make you miss out on this great blessing. Keep on praising Him in a wholehearted manner, knowing that Jesus receives your praise as a sweet perfume. In fact, God feeds on our praise.

◗ Suddenly, you will feel joy that gradually increases until your whole body is overwhelmed with an incomprehensible feeling of delight. At that moment you will be baptised and sealed with the Holy Spirit! You will start to speak a completely different language, and though you will not be able to understand it, you will not want to stop speaking it.

Do not be afraid. The Lord Jesus Himself said that if a son asks his father for bread, he will not receive a stone (Luke 11:9-13). In the same way, if we who are God's children ask Him for the Holy Spirit, He will not allow a different spirit to enter us.

When a person is baptised in the Holy Spirit, he immediately receives God's life-force, which enables him to fight and overcome any battle. The Holy Spirit helps us to seal off any openings that the devil could use to enter and attack us. As a result, we are fully able to carry out God's will.

If you want to be baptised in the Holy Spirit, pay very close attention to the words of Ms Gordon Lindsay, who asked, 'How can a person be filled with the Holy Spirit?' Let us start with a frequently quoted Pentecostal passage of the Bible, which says, *"And they were all filled with the Holy Spirit and began to speak with other tongues, as the Spirit gave them utterance."* (Acts 2:4)

Who began to speak? Some will say it was the Holy Spirit. But, this is not what the Holy Scriptures say. Read the verse again: "And they were all filled with the Holy Spirit and (they) began to speak with other tongues…"

Someone once said, 'Well, if it is me who speaks, then it is my flesh who speaks.' Of course it is your flesh! Until such day when you acquire an immortal body, it is your flesh that speaks. The supernatural part was that they spoke "as the Spirit gave them utterance." This means that if you had to think about what you were going to say, there would be nothing supernatural in it.

After you have expelled all unwelcome thoughts from your mind and are concentrating on the Lord in prayer, you will begin, by faith, to say words that will come out of the depths of your heart. You will not understand them, but this does not really matter. And do not worry about what it will sound like when you begin to speak these strange words. In the beginning, they might sound like the words of a child learning to speak, as we read in Isaiah 28:11: *"For with stammering lips and another tongue He will speak to this people."*

Do not hesitate. Take a deep breath and start to speak in tongues. Clearly pronounce the words that God puts in your heart, bearing in mind that when a person is saved, Christ is inside of him. The Bible affirms, *"For in Him dwells all the fullness of the Godhead bodily."* (Colossians 2:9) Believe that you have the Holy Spirit and take action. It is your turn to act, not God's.

When you speak a language, you use your tongue, mouth and throat. To speak in tongues you have to do exactly the same thing. We have spoken to many people who have felt very stressed out when seeking the Holy Spirit. Their lips are so stiff that they are not able to speak even their own language.

Be at rest with the Lord. Relax your muscles and allow the Holy Spirit to do His wonderful work in your life.

You may know English, Portuguese, French, German, Spanish or any number of languages, but you can only speak one of them at a time. And so, if you insist on speaking your own language when seeking the baptism, you can pray until the Day of Judgment, but you will never speak in tongues.

Praise the Lord for a few minutes and when you feel the presence of the Holy Spirit, stop speaking your own language and start, by faith, to speak in tongues. The moment you respond to the touch of the Holy Spirit, you will feel a great joy filling your soul, for the Bible says, *"And the disciples were filled with joy and with the Holy Spirit."* (Acts 13:52) At times this joy is felt only some days after the baptism occurs, which is an indication of when that person has learned to submit to the Spirit.

Where is the best place to receive the Holy Spirit? The majority of people receive Him in the church, since it is a place where people feel motivated to praise and worship the Lord – an indispensable requirement for the baptism. And yet, there are exceptions to every rule. For instance, a lorry driver once testified that he had been baptised while driving. He was so happy, that he pulled over and started to jump for joy beside the vehicle; another gentleman told us that he had received the baptism while he was shaving; another said that he was in bed when it happened. Many have written to us saying that they had been baptised in prison. There was even a lady who said that she received the baptism while doing her washing, and, according to the Bible, the 120 people who received the baptism in the Holy Spirit in the Upper Room were sitting down (Acts 2:2). This means that God does not necessarily prefer any particular place or body position.

What we have to understand is that the baptism in the Holy Spirit is an extremely important step for any true Christian to achieve the fullness of life and communion with God. When a person allows Him into his life, this person is ready to overcome the spiritual hosts of wickedness at work in this world.

The fruit of the Holy Spirit

The Bible considers the fruit (Galatians 5:22) of the Holy Spirit as one single gift, a package if you will. The Holy Spirit gives these qualities to followers of the Lord Jesus Christ as a complete set, as though they were only one quality. As a consequence, all nine form part of that person's spiritual development, so that Christians *"may be filled with all the fullness of God."* (Ephesians 3:19)

Obviously, the fruit of the Spirit is the result of the Holy Spirit's work in the lives of those who submit to the will of the Lord, and is produced by Him, and Him alone. No one can bear this fruit by themselves – the involvement of the Holy Spirit is imperative.

On the other hand, the Holy Spirit does not force His fruit on anyone. A person must first manifest a strong desire for the will of God to be done in his life; only then will the Holy Spirit come and transform him completely.

Fruit is the result of what is planted; it can be good or bad, depending on the seed that is sown. And so, if we want the fruit of the Spirit, the divine thoughts of the Holy Bible must be sown in our hearts.

The Word of God, which is the mind of Christ, has to be planted deep in the hearts of those who want the Holy Spirit to produce His fruit in them. For example, when good seed is sown, it dies only to spring to life again and produce the intended fruit. This miracle of reproduction is the result of a connection between God and nature, and is precisely what happens to Christians. They die to the world and to their own desires in order to live for God and produce the fruit of the Holy Spirit, which is: love, joy, peace, longsuffering, kindness, goodness, faithfulness, gentleness and self-control.

LOVE

We will first focus on love because it is the foundation of this set. All the other fruits are built and developed from love.

Basically, love is to want others to have what we want for ourselves. It is to spend time and energy on behalf of others, just as we voluntarily spend time and energy on ourselves. The cross itself symbolises true love: the vertical bar representing our love for God, and the horizontal bar representing our love for others.

In love we find God's greatest commandment:

"You shall love the LORD your God with all your heart, with all your soul, and with all your mind. This is the first and great commandment. And the second is like it: You shall love your neighbor as yourself."

Matthew 22:37-40

When there is love in a relationship, there is a natural give and take – much more than compassion and affection. A person who loves is unconcerned about himself, and sacrifices without any selfish interest. Personally, I believe that loving is giving.

The different kinds of love:

Self-love – Although the Holy Scriptures do not condemn this kind of love, it has to be closely monitored to assure that it does not turn into selfish obsession.

Love of God – Love for God, for the Lord Jesus and for things above should be evident in our lives. In fact, this is God's first and greatest commandment (Matthew 22:37).

God's love for man – This is the source of all goodness and the guideline for our relationships with others.

Our love for others – God demands this love, as He makes clear in the second greatest commandment (Matthew 22:39).

JOY

Joy is by definition a feeling of contentment, satisfaction, great happiness or rejoicing.

But joy as a quality of the Holy Spirit in the life of a Christian is much more than mere feelings. It is a never-ending sense of happiness brought on by the assurance that the Spirit of God is living within us. It is the result of hearing and accepting the Gospel (Luke 2:10) and of the salvation experience. It is constant, refusing to be affected by the disappointments of this world.

On the other hand, the joy of a non-Christian is caused by comical situations, positive physical experiences and the like, and is therefore inconstant. It is a temporary sensation that is easily overcome by the sadness of this world.

One of our greatest sources of joy is the fact that the Lord makes a distinction between His people and the people of this world. In fact, He Himself experiences joy, as it is written, *"Do not sorrow, for the joy of the LORD is your strength."* (Nehemiah 8:10)

When a person has joy, he is spiritually sound, which is only possible when he has developed a true relationship with God. Joy is to rejoice in the Holy Spirit. God does not tolerate discouragement, quite to the contrary. His Word admonishes us saying, *"Serve the LORD with gladness; come before His presence with singing."* (Psalm 100:2) and, *"Let the hearts of those rejoice who seek the LORD!"* (Psalm 105:3)

For this reason, the order of the day is to rejoice in the Lord. It is a gift of God that keeps us focused on the fact that He is on the throne and that everything is under His control. Joy not only gives us hope and courage, it reveals our trust in the Lord Jesus and the gladness we have in living for Him.

PEACE

Man's fall in the Garden of Eden put an end to his inner peace and to the peaceful relationship he had with God, with others and with nature. However, God re-established that peace through the sacrifice of the Lord Jesus, as it is written, *"Therefore, having been justified by faith, we have peace with God through our Lord Jesus Christ."* (Romans 5:1)

Peace is more than the ability to remain calm in times of great confusion. It is the spiritual quality that comes from being reconciled with God, forgiven of our sins and converted. The Lord Jesus said, *"Peace I leave with you, My peace I give to you; not as the world gives do I give to you."* (John 14:27)

This peace is a gift from the Holy Spirit. In the same way that the Spirit teaches us about Christ, He gives us the serenity to face hardships. As a result, the Holy Spirit is called the Helper. We are able to remain calm in difficult times because the Holy Spirit renews our trust in the Lord Jesus and fills us with His inexpressible peace. Peace is the opposite of hatred, dissension, disputes, conflict, envy and all other works of the flesh. As a child nestles in his mother's arms, so Christians find peace in Jesus – real peace!

Peace is precious. Those who find it are happy, and those who do not are miserable. God gave us His Son in order to set us free from our enemy. Human beings usually look for peace in the material things of this world, not realising that these things always bring more anxiety and confusion. There has always been a lack of peace, of harmony and goodwill among the people in this world. But this is not a part of God's plan.

More than ever, we are affected by this sad state of affairs. Various worldwide organisations assure us that they have the understanding and cooperation of the countries of the world; and yet, we see little result from their well-intentioned efforts. Why is this? If we search the Word of God we will learn that a person can only have peace when he surrenders his life to God and gives Him the glory that He rightly deserves (see Luke 2).

When Christ was born, angels sang praises to God, saying: *"Glory to God in the highest, and on earth peace, goodwill towards men!"* (Luke 2:14) But as long as humans refuse to live a life of submission to and harmony with God, they will experience serious conflicts within and without. Those who do not live in harmony with God are incapable of bringing peace to others, since they themselves have no peace. They are totally unable to reach out and bring peace to those around them.

No one can give what he does not have (Luke 6:43-45). Peace is a state of the soul; it consists of living in harmony with yourself and with God. Those who are at peace with their Creator will also be at peace with themselves, and will live in peace with others.

The lack of peace in this world and the divisions that exist in the church today, reflect our situation before God. We make a big mistake when we try to control everything around us, or when we do things for personal fame and glory. There are many people, including some who profess to believe in the name of the Lord, who trust in the work of their own hands. There are still others who turn to philosophy, science and other sources of human wisdom in an effort to find inner peace.

Peace is one of the most glorious gifts of the Holy Spirit. Without God there is no peace! Without the presence of the Prince of Peace, of whom the prophet Isaiah speaks, there is no love. Before Jesus left His disciples, He said to them, "Peace I leave with you, My peace I give to you." If we believe this promise, we will be able to live out the rest of this verse from the Bible, which says, *"Let not your heart be troubled, neither let it be afraid."* (John 14:27)

LONG-SUFFERING

A long-suffering person is patient even in the face of continual provocations and insults. God's long-suffering character, for example, is what allows Him to patiently tolerate the iniquity of mankind, resisting the impulse to fly into a rage and annihilate the entire human race. Though humans are constantly making mistakes and committing sins, God remains patient and merciful because of His love.

When we acquire this quality, we are able to tolerate the most aggravating situations because we know that the Lord Jesus is tolerant towards our own sins.

KINDNESS

A person with this quality has an excellent character. You would never characterise a kind person as inflexible or demanding; on the contrary, he makes an effort to be kind to everyone. And yet, we do, on occasion, find new-converts who have an inflexible attitude towards others.

A kind person is a mediator, is compliant, flexible and meek, and in so doing impresses those around him.

GOODNESS

Similar to kindness, a person with this quality is generous, does not hesitate to help others or to live by the law of love. The Parable of the Good Samaritan (Luke 10:30-35) is an excellent example of goodness.

A good person is unconcerned about himself and does not expect anything in return for his acts of goodness. He does not allow a person's colour, gender, appearance or financial situation to affect him. Rather, he delights in glorifying the Lord Jesus through acts of generosity.

FAITHFULNESS

In Greek, faithfulness denotes an attitude of 'trust' and 'loyalty'. Therefore, a person who is faithful to the Lord Jesus will manifest loyalty and unconditional trust in Him.

When a person is converted to the Lord Jesus, from that moment on, his soul is totally dependent on Him. Both trust and faith enable this person to remain faithful to Him.

Many Christians are faithful to the Lord Jesus only when they have money, their family is healthy and things are running smoothly. This kind of person is loyal to the Lord in the same way that Peter was. When hard times come – persecution, financial problems, etc. – they take their eyes off the Author and Finisher of their faith and look at the circumstances. This leads to frustration and sadness, and eventually to unfaithfulness – a clear sign of doubt and uncertainty.

When things are fine, who cannot be faithful? But when things are bad, faithfulness to God requires sacrifice. In exchange for our faithfulness to Him, the Holy Spirit gives us the power to overcome any and all obstacles.

God is always testing our faithfulness. For this reason, Christians need to keep their spiritual eyes wide open to avoid missing out on the gift of the Holy Spirit.

GENTLENESS

The Lord Jesus said, *"Blessed are the meek, for they shall inherit the earth."* (Matthew 5:5) *"Take My yoke upon you and learn from Me, for I am gentle and lowly in heart, and you will find rest for your souls."* (Matthew 11:29)

Gentleness is a mildness of character which causes a person to submit to God and, consequently, to others. In addition to the Lord Jesus, Moses is a good example of gentleness: *"Now the man Moses was very humble, more than all men who were on the face of the earth."* (Numbers 12:3)

Gentleness is derived from true humility, and a person who is truly humble recognises the worth of those around him, refusing to indulge in an attitude of superiority. Had the Lord Jesus not manifested this virtue, He would never have tolerated the insults and mocking of those around Him. His meek spirit overcame the temptation to lash out at those who intentionally provoked Him.

SELF-CONTROL

This fruit of the Holy Spirit enables us to subdue the impulses of the flesh, which always lead to death. Discipline is vital for the Christian who wants to achieve victory through the Lord Jesus.

We live in a hostile world, where what is wrong is considered right, and vice-versa. We live on this planet, but we do not belong to it. We have to obey certain laws of this world even when they are contrary to the laws that rule our lives. We are constantly being confronted by situations in which, depending on the attitude we take, we either glorify our Lord or put Him to shame.

Proverbs 16:32 says that he who rules his spirit is better than he who takes a city. In fact, the worst battle is that of a man against his own fleshly desires. If it were not for the Holy Spirit, Christians would be completely unable to control themselves.

When the apostle Paul spoke about the conflict between the flesh and the Holy Spirit (Galatians 5:16-21), he was not referring to our physical body. The flesh he mentioned is our natural instincts and desires that are truly against the Spirit of God, and it is we who are responsible to control them.

The Bible contains two main doctrines: the Law and the Gospel.

The Law

Through the Law God gave instructions on how to live, what to do and what not to do. Therefore, when a person lives by the Laws and commandments of the Old Testament, he is saved by the good works that he does (Leviticus 19:2,3; Deuteronomy 6:6,7).

It is extremely difficult for a person to be saved through the Law, because even when he has faithfully fulfilled the vast majority of the Law, he will be considered a failure when one small thing is left out. And yet, there are many modern-day churches who legalistically demand that their members practise the Law, as with Sabbatarians, who force their followers to keep the Sabbath, one of God's commands. In fact, every religion or denomination whose faith is based on the Law ends up encouraging superficial, antichristian behaviour, because they ignore that the just must live by faith in the Lord Jesus Christ (Hebrews 10:38).

Had the Law been able to save mankind, the Lord Jesus' physical life would have been absolutely pointless. This does not mean that the Law was wrong or flawed. Rather, it was created to prepare and discipline the Jewish people for the coming of the Lord Jesus – to prepare their rebellious, hard hearts.

The Gospel

The Gospel stands for good news. By it we receive salvation through faith in the One who perfectly obeyed the Law in every way without fail, down to the last command: the Lord Jesus Christ. The Law teaches us what must and must not be done, while the Gospel teaches us what God has done – and will do – through His Son Jesus.

The Gospel brings the fruit of the Holy Spirit, God's grace, to all who put their faith in the Lord Jesus. It brings the Holy Spirit and His fruit so that God's church may grow.

Those who live by the Law and the commandments will not benefit from the fruit of the Holy Spirit since they believe that they can be good Christians by their willpower – which is in fact impossible without the help of the Holy Spirit.

Demons and tongues

BLASPHEMY

Many people have been deceived because of a lack of understanding about tongues. They accept the Lord Jesus as Saviour and insist that they are baptised in the Holy Spirit, and yet their lives are worse than they have ever been.

Demons are able to manifest by speaking in false tongues – imitating those who are baptised in the Holy Spirit. At the same time, many longstanding members of churches are anxious to speak in tongues and want the baptism at any cost just because so-and-so, who is new in the church, has already been baptised with the Spirit of God. Instead of worshipping the Lord Jesus with sincere hearts, they obsess about speaking in tongues. Little do they know that their selfish behaviour is an open door for the devil to come in and deceive them into speaking in false tongues, convincing them that they have been baptised in the Holy Spirit.

Later on, rotten fruit begins to show. Instead of happiness and joy, they are plagued by bad moods and complain about every little thing; nothing seems to please them. They are like weeds among the wheat. Their behaviour causes confusion, especially when they are allowed to make false prophecies in and around the church, criticising the pastor and spreading rebellion among the congregation.

Tongues do exist. People who are baptised in the Holy Spirit speak in tongues. However, not everyone who speaks in tongues is baptised in the Holy Spirit.

One of the gifts of the Holy Spirit is spiritual discernment. In our years of ministry, we have witnessed many who were deceived by the devil. I remember a lady who came to me on one occasion, saying that she was filled with the Holy Spirit. Although she was very excited, I was not too sure about her "filling". One day, she began to sing a song that was so beautiful and unusual that anyone hearing her would immediately assume that she was indeed filled with the Holy Spirit. A few days later, she got sick and I decided to visit her. While I was praying for her, asking God to deliver her from any and all evil, a demonic spirit manifested and began to sing that very same unusual song. The spirit called itself the "black lyricist".

Many think they are baptised in the Holy Spirit when, in fact, they have an evil spirit. However, as long as a person is sincere, he will soon be delivered.

Deceiving spirits cannot resist the presence of God; they always manifest their true character in the end. As a result, the power of God is able to come in and deliver that person.

CAN A CHRISTIAN WHO HAS BEEN BAPTISED HAVE DEMONS?

No part of the Holy Scriptures suggests that a person who is baptised in the Holy Spirit can have demons. When a person is baptised in the Holy Spirit, he is sealed by God and, as a result, demons can no longer enter his body. As the Bible affirms, we are the temple of the Holy Spirit – He will never agree to share His temple with a demonic spirit.

However, it is important to remember that our status before God is not absolute, we have to constantly be on the watch. Though the baptism in the Holy Spirit places a person under God's grace, that person is still able to fall into sin, deny Jesus and resist the Holy Spirit; and, in so doing, lose the Holy Spirit and open himself to the work of the devil.

This is exactly what happened to Saul. He had been filled with the Holy Spirit, but lost God's grace when he disobeyed. He consulted an unclean spirit that lied to him and made him believe that it was the spirit of the prophet Samuel. As a consequence, the end of his life was truly terrible.

Anyone seeking the Holy Spirit in a careless way runs the serious risk of being deceived by a demon. One day I was praying for a group of people in a particular meeting and commanded the demon that had been passing itself off as the Holy Spirit to leave their lives. To my surprise, people who seemed to be delivered manifested the most terrible demons.

Although the Bible does not teach that speaking in tongues is a requirement of the baptism in the Holy Spirit, Bible references show that speaking in tongues was common among people who were baptised in the Holy Spirit. For example:

The Jews on the Day of Pentecost (Acts 2:4)

The Romans in the house of Cornelius (Acts 10:46)

The Greeks in Ephesus (Acts 19:6)

THE ATTITUDES OF A PERSON
WHO IS BAPTISED IN THE HOLY SPIRIT

I have watched people being baptised in the Holy Spirit and have noticed that after the baptism, every one of them is filled with love, peace and joy, whilst retaining full conscience and control of themselves. I say this because there are many sincere people whose emotions are entirely out of control when they are supposedly baptised in the Holy Spirit. Some actually fall to the ground, are thrown into fits of shaking and draw unnecessary attention to themselves. In these cases, what we are witnessing is not the baptism in the Holy Spirit, but a fleshly, demonic manifestation, which disturbs those who are eager and willing to receive the presence of God.

When a person is baptised in the Holy Spirit, it is perfectly natural for him to feel like crying, smiling or singing for joy. What is not natural, however, is for him to lose consciousness – a characteristic of demonic manifestation. The Holy Spirit never leads a person to a state of unconsciousness.

THE PURPOSE OF THE HOLY SPIRIT

When a person is baptised in the Holy Spirit, his attitudes and goals are completely changed because he is now a person that God has called to do His holy will.

The Lord Jesus never seals a person with the Holy Spirit for no reason; quite to the contrary, there is always a purpose behind this experience. If a person accepts God's calling and allows His will to be done in his life, not only will he be happy, but also make all those who hear his testimony about Jesus happy.

The Lord can only manifest in this world through people who are filled with His Spirit. This is precisely why people are baptised in the Holy Spirit.

One of the greatest obstacles to the baptism is that people's objectives differ from God's. Many seek the baptism without ever intending to serve the Lord, and others want the baptism for prideful reasons, to appear spiritual to those around them.

A person's motives will determine whether or not he receives the baptism in the Holy Spirit. We advise those who have been seeking the baptism for a long time to stop and ask themselves if they are seeking the baptism to please God or to please their own fleshly and demonic instincts – to do their own will or the will of Him who called them.

No one wants us to receive the baptism in the Holy Spirit more than the Lord Jesus Christ Himself, for it was He who said, *"However, when He, the Spirit of truth, has come, He will guide you into all truth; for He will not speak on His own authority, but whatever He hears He will speak; and He will tell you things to come. He will glorify Me, for He will take of what is Mine and declare it to you."*

John 16:13,14

With greater numbers of people being baptised in the Holy Spirit, greater numbers of people will come to know the Lord Jesus and His plan for humanity, because spiritual things are discerned spiritually, that is, through the Holy Spirit.

The greatest desire of those who are baptised in the Holy Spirit

Without a doubt, the main characteristic of a person who is baptised in the Holy Spirit is the love he has for others. This love surpasses all personal interests and is the greatest of all Christian principles. It is much more than feelings of friendship or kindness; rather, it is a strong desire to rescue people from the pit that they are in and lead them to salvation through the Lord Jesus Christ, to newness of life, communion with God and eternal sanctification.

When a person manifests a sincere desire to win souls for the Kingdom of God, the baptism in the Holy Spirit is closer than he might think.

Blasphemy against the Holy Spirit: the unforgivable sin

The Holy Spirit convicts us of sin and reveals the Saviour to us. But whenever a person acts disrespectfully towards the Holy Spirit and blasphemes His name, He will depart and that person will no longer have anyone to convict him of his sins.

Whether a person is religious or not, everyone has faith, and when faith is placed in the Living God, a blessed life is the result. The Holy Spirit gives us faith. But when a person blasphemes against the Holy Spirit, God's Spirit departs from him and he becomes spiritually cold; in other words, that person will no longer have the motivation to seek the presence of God because God no longer means anything to him. This is why the Lord Jesus warns us, saying, "*Assuredly, I say to you, all sins will be forgiven the sons of men, and whatever blasphemies they may utter; but he who blasphemes against the Holy Spirit never has forgiveness, but is subject to eternal condemnation."* (Mark 3:28,29)

Sin against the Father and the Son can be forgiven because it is the Holy Spirit who guides us to repentance. But who is left to guide a person to repentance when he has sinned against the Spirit Himself?

The gifts of the Holy Spirit

Before we begin the study of the gifts of the Holy Spirit, it is important to understand that the gifts belong exclusively to the Holy Spirit. This means that no one owns any of the gifts.

Many sincere Christians, without knowing much about the Word of God, think they have the gift of prophecy. The fact that they have been used to prophesy does not mean that this gift is theirs to keep. If that were true, the work of the Holy Spirit in our lives would be limited. If they say, for example, that they possess the gift of prophecy, then no one else could have that gift besides them. The Holy Spirit would then be forced to search for someone else through whom He could manifest His other gifts.

The truth is that the gifts of the Holy Spirit are given according to the need. For example, I know a man of God who has been used many times by the Holy Spirit to prophesy about things that would happened at a later time. And yet, this does not mean that he owns that gift.

The gifts of the Holy Spirit are distributed as the Spirit desires, in accordance to the needs of the Church of the Lord Jesus Christ. A person can be used to speak words of wisdom, to perform miracles or to discern spirits; it all depends on the circumstances.

The people of God must understand that it is His Spirit who guides the Church of the Lord Jesus, and that, whenever it is needed, He chooses someone whose heart is concerned about His Work so that He can use him.

The Lord Jesus guides His Church through the Holy Spirit; and the Holy Spirit entrusts His gifts only to people who truly love Him.

THE WORD OF WISDOM

This gift has to do with the ability to understand the mysteries of the Holy Spirit and pass them on to others; that is, the ability to understand Christianity and transmit this understanding to others.

The Word of God is spirit and life (John 6:63). As a consequence we need wisdom to understand it and to avoid misinterpretation of it. Many have abandoned faith after giving ear to deceiving spirits and doctrines of demons (1 Timothy 4:1).

Whenever we need to make a decision about a difficult case, the Holy Spirit gives us discernment of God's will through His Word so that we can do it in a wise manner. This is what happened to Solomon when he judged a case between two women (1 Kings 3:16-28). At that moment, the word of wisdom was entrusted to Solomon in the form of a gift of the Spirit so that he could bring justice to his people. This gift is extremely important because it ensures justice for the people of God.

THE WORD OF KNOWLEDGE

This gift has to do with what we learn and pass on to others. It has nothing to do with worldly knowledge, if it did, this gift of the Holy Spirit would not be necessary. The gift of knowledge is the ability to understand things that are unknown to the natural man, yet revealed to those who belong to the Kingdom of God. The word of knowledge is passed on to the followers of the Lord Jesus day by day, little by little.

Take, for example, the many verses in the Bible. There are things in the Bible that can only be understood through prayer and fasting. And that is precisely when we need the word of knowledge, which is given by the Holy Spirit only to those who desire it in order to benefit others, and nothing else.

FAITH

This gift should not be mistaken for the faith that justifies (Romans 5:1). Rather, it is the manifestation of a deep trust in God that makes the impossible become possible, and this, through the direct action of the Holy Spirit in the lives of Christians who are eager for the Word of God.

The Holy Spirit pours out this gift, in particular, on those who are humble in spirit, accept His Word in their hearts and act upon it – people who have rebelled against religions that refuse to approach the Holy Bible in a straightforward manner.

In fact, true Christians seek to understand the Word of God as it really is, and strive to present it to others in the same way. They are determined to practise it at any cost because they understand that what is written there will surely be fulfilled. It is only waiting for someone, moved by the gift of faith, to implement it.

When the Lord Jesus spoke to the fig tree (Mark 11:14) He used the gift of faith; Peter used the same gift to heal a lame man (Acts 3:6); in the same manner, the Holy Spirit used Paul to heal a man crippled from his mother's womb, a man who had never walked (Acts 14:8-10).

We should not limit the gift of faith to healing and performing miracles. It should also be used to help Christians endure the afflictions that the world imposes on them, in the same way the Lord did. That was the case of Antipas (Revelation 2:13), who according to some historians, was locked inside a bronze image of a bull and thrown into a blazing fire. Antipas endured that painful death for the love of the Lord Jesus Christ. At the time, the Emperor Domitian had made a decree that all nations should worship him as though he were God. Those who resisted his decree were killed in cruel ways. Antipas was just one of his many victims.

Through the centuries, many men of God changed the course of history through the gift of faith:

"...*who through faith subdued kingdoms, worked righteousness, obtained promises, stopped the mouths of lions, quenched the violence of fire, escaped the edge of the sword, out of weakness were made strong, became valiant in battle, turned to flight the armies of the aliens. Women received their dead raised to life again. Others were tortured, not accepting deliverance, that they might obtain a better resurrection. Still others had trial of mockings and scourgings, yes, and of chains and imprisonment. They were stoned, they were sawn in two, were tempted, were slain with the sword. They wandered about in sheepskins and goatskins, being destitute, afflicted, tormented – of whom the world was not worthy. They wandered in deserts and mountains, in dens and caves of the earth."*

Hebrews 11:33-38

As we can see, the gift of faith is characterised by the actions of a men who are filled with the Holy Spirit.

HEALING

Through the sacrifice of the Lord Jesus we have the right to divine healing. This is not a matter of having faith, but rather of a sick person accepting the sacrifice of the Lord on the cross, for by His stripes we are healed (Isaiah 53:5). This means that we have already been healed, and as a result do not need to keep asking for what has already been given to us.

The gift of healing is given to pastors to help those who are unable to believe due to a physical impairment, and as a consequence, are unable to take possession of what God has given them. There are people, for example, who cannot hear the Word of God because they are deaf.

The healing of a man who was deaf and had a speech impediment in Mark 7:32-35 is an example of the manifestation of this gift in the ministry of the Lord Jesus. He could not hear about the Kingdom of God or of the blessings of God, and yet, through the gift of healing the Lord Himself caused him to hear and speak freely.

The gift of healing does not depend on the sick person's faith. This gift is like an electric shock that strikes the sick and heals them regardless of the condition they are in.

The working of miracles

The fifth of nine gifts of the Holy Spirit, a miracle is by definition an event that appears to be contrary to the laws of nature and regarded as an act of God. Note that all the gifts of the Holy Spirit are regarded as miracles – they are the work of God manifesting in His servants throughout the world.

This ministry has to do with supernatural events such as the following list, taken from the Old Testament:

◗ The Red Sea was parted (Exodus 14:21)

◗ The waters of Marah became sweet (Exodus 12:25)

◗ Water came out of the rock at Rephidim (Exodus 17:6)

◗ Water came out of the rock at Meribah (Numbers 20:11)

◗ The Jordan was parted (Joshua 3:16)

◗ The sun and the moon stood still (Joshua 10:13)

◗ The prophet Elijah called down fire from heaven on Mount Carmel (1Kings 18:38)

And from the New Testament:

◗ Water turned into wine (John 2:9)

◗ The calming of a great storm (Matthew 8:26)

◗ Jesus walked on the water (Matthew 14:25)

◗ Prison doors were opened (Acts 5:19)

◗ Peter was set free from prison (Acts 12:7)

These miracles, as well as many others that were performed, broke the laws of nature. They are true manifestations of the working of miracles, which only happens according to God's will and the immediate needs of the moment, for the honour and glory of God.

That was the case of Joshua, who needed to cross the Jordan River to reach the city of Jericho (Joshua 6). In this, and in some other cases in the Bible, the working of miracles was essential to resolve an immediate problem.

Another great example of the manifestation of this gift is the UCKG, which exists thanks to the working of wonders the Holy Spirit performs through His servants.

PROPHECY

For the majority of Christians this is the most mysterious of all the gifts, and in particular for those who are anxious to use it in their ministry. A lack of information about this gift has brought about the spiritual and physical destruction of thousands who listened to false prophets.

This ministry is more popular among women, due to the fact that they are more receptive, docile and sensitive; and for the very same reason, they are also deceived more easily. Remember Eve who listened to the serpent; Sarah who convinced Abraham to sleep with her maidservant; Delilah, who shaved off Samson's hair and took his strength away from him. I believe that the lack of opportunities in the church, combined with a lack of sound guidance, make them easy prey to deceiving spirits.

It is important to say that this ministry does not belong to people, but to the Holy Spirit, and is entrusted to people according to His will.

The ministry of prophecy was widely used in the formation of the nation of Israel. At that time, God revealed Himself to His people exclusively through prophets, who were anointed for this purpose, as is written in Hebrews 1:1,2.

"God, who in various times and in various ways spoke in times past to the fathers by the prophets, has in these last days spoken to us by His Son…"

In those days, it was common for people to seek out prophets whenever they needed to know the will and plans of God for a particular situation. The kings of Israel would normally consult the prophets to know whether or not they should go to war against other nations (see 2 Chronicles 18:14).

In a time that the Bible did not yet exist, and the Holy Spirit had not yet been given as a guide, it was necessary to seek advice from prophets (John 16.13). By the grace of God, we who are alive today do not need to consult prophets to receive a special revelation from God, because the Lord Jesus has sent the Spirit of Truth to prevent us from getting lost in the vastness of His Word, and to give us His light as a guide.

I know a man who spent years sitting in a church pew listening to the most beautiful sermons. He was waiting for the day that his pastor would be used by the Holy Spirit to prophesy and tell him what to do with his life. Meanwhile, he constantly attended informal prayer meetings in the hope that one day someone there would have a direct revelation from God for him. For years this man lived a very limited life simply because he refused to accept what was already revealed in the Holy Scriptures.

There are many young new converts who are desperate for a prophetic word that will give them direction for their lives, and when they do not receive one, they lose all desire to do the will of God because they wrongly think that He does not care about them.

Sometimes, the devil makes people who want to do the Work of God feel discouraged for not knowing what God wants from them, when, in fact, God's desire to use them is crystal clear in the Bible.

Those who are obsessed with receiving a particular revelation from God through prophecy will always be disappointed, because in the end a Christian shall live by faith (Galatians 3:11).

The Word of God is a living prophecy, and those who accept it by faith and truly desire to do the will of God must practise it. Faith is action! Read James 2:14-16. Consecrating yourself through prayer, fasting and the reading of the Bible is useless unless you practise the Word of God. The Lord Jesus Himself admonishes us to practise His Word in Matthew 7:24-27.

I believe wholeheartedly that God's Word would have long ago lost its value and would no longer exist if God had wanted us to live by personal prophecies. An absurd idea! Likewise, it would be absurd for us to base our lives on the prophecies of a handful of 'more consecrated' sisters.

It reminds me of a church where a lady dedicated herself to prayer and fasting. During prayer meetings the pastor would even allow her to make the service. In fact, her prayers seemed far more fervent than other people's prayers, and after long periods of prayer and some speaking in tongues, she would always prophesy. This made her a highly respected member of that congregation.

One day, however, she decided to move in with her unbelieving boyfriend. Just think of how many people had listened to her words, taken them to heart and were deceived by the unclean spirit controlling that church.

People usually want to see first in order to believe in the Word of God. And yet, the same people quickly accept prophecies from tarot card and palm readers, horoscopes, crystals, personal church prophecies, etc. Little do they know that this is Satan's favourite ministry, and that psychiatric wards are packed with people who similarly listened to the devil's voice.

You might think that we are totally against prophecy, but that is not true. Who are we to judge the Word of God? Prophecy as a gift does exist and must always agree with the Bible, abiding by divine discipline, just as everything else that comes from God.

A prophecy is a prediction about the future made by an anointed prophet of the Lord or by someone that the Holy Spirit chooses for that particular purpose. A prophecy can never contradict the Bible, because the One that speaks through the Bible is the same One that speaks through a prophet. An anointed prophet or someone who receives such gift will never make a statement that disagrees with the Bible. The intention of a person who prophesies should be to benefit the Church of the Lord Jesus Christ, to edify, exhort and comfort the Church. These must be the sole objectives of a prophecy (1Corinthians 14:3).

Prophets and people who prophesy (note that not everyone who prophesies is necessarily a prophet, and not every prophet prophesies) will never prophesy to one particular person. There is only one New Testament example of a prophet prophesying to one particular person (Acts 21:11) and that example cannot be made into a general rule.

So far, we have dealt with prophecy in a narrower sense, the biblical sense. If we spoke about prophecy in general we would have to agree that a person does not need to be a prophet, or even inspired by God, to predict the future. Through study and careful observation, one person can predict another person's future with a small margin of error – as with weather and financial forecasts.

Obviously, a prophet in the biblical sense is much more than a predictor of the future. He is an individual bestowed with a spiritual gift to teach, and whenever he does predict the future, it is for a very good reason and always inspired by the Holy Spirit.

The example of the prophet Agabus, who proclaimed by the power of the Spirit that there was going to be a widespread famine throughout the world (Acts 11:28), reveals God's desire to warn His people about future events. The book of Revelation itself is a perfect prophecy, whose aim is to edify, exhort, comfort and prepare the people of God for the events that will precede the second coming of the Lord Jesus Christ.

Another aspect of prophecies is that everyone who announces the gospel of the Lord Jesus Christ is, in fact, prophesying. To affirm that the Lord Jesus heals all kinds of diseases, sets people free from the oppression of the devil, brings prosperity and saves lives, is nothing less than prophesying that these things will happen in the lives of those who believe in this prophetic word, which is the Word of God.

With the number of prophecies growing by the day, here is some useful advice that will happen Christians identify when a prophecy is from God and when it is from the devil:

◗ When you hear a prophecy you must first ask yourself if it is in agreement with the Bible, that is, if it edifies, exhorts and comforts the church as a whole.

◗ If a prophecy is for a specific person or a specific group of people, it is false.

◗ You should wait to see if the prophecy is fulfilled or not. If what was prophesied actually happens, it is true and comes from God; if it does not, it is false and demonic.

◗ A close look at the life of a prophet or messenger will also help you decide whether or not to accept his prophecies, as it is written:

"Beware of false prophets, who come to you in sheep's clothing, but inwardly they are ravenous wolves. You will know them by their fruits. Do men gather grapes from thornbushes or figs from thistles? Even so, every good tree bears good fruit, but a bad tree bears bad fruit. A good tree cannot bear bad fruit, nor can a bad tree bear good fruit. Every tree that does not bear good fruit is cut down and thrown into the fire. Therefore by their fruits you will know them."

Matthew 7:15-20

In the Primitive Church, there were many non-Christians who had psychic and spiritual powers. They were widely used by deceiving spirits, which did not manifest in the same way they do today. At that time, deceiving spirits would enter people's lives without being noticed and, through them, cause extraordinary things to happen. When Moses and Aaron went to speak to Pharaoh as the Lord had commanded, Aaron threw down his rod in front of Pharaoh and it became a snake. At that point Pharaoh called in the wise men and sorcerers of Egypt and they did the same thing with their enchantments (Exodus 7:10,11).

This reveals the degree to which deceiving spirits can perform wonders to catch people's attention and, most importantly, gain their belief and trust.

In order to give His Church a solid base of faith to build upon, the Lord Jesus gave His followers, through the Holy Spirit, the ability to discern spirits. In this way they were empowered to distinguish between those who were from God and those whose speech and actions were inspired by the devil.

It is important to know the difference between right and wrong. And yet it is not always easy, therefore this gift from the Holy Spirit is crucial in assuring that the right decisions are made. The Bible says, *"The heart is deceitful above all things, and desperately wicked; who can know it? I, the LORD search the heart, I test the mind, even to give every man according to his ways, according to the fruits of his doings."*

Jeremiah 17:9,10

We frequently come across sincere people with a desire to do what is right, and yet, upon closer examination, discover that unclean spirits are hiding behind their good deeds. Not everything that we consider good, is good in God's eyes. Many times we are convinced that what we are doing is right and good, only to find out later that it was wrong. This is why we so clearly need this gift.

The apostle John gives us a stern warning about this, saying: *"Beloved, do not believe every spirit, but test the spirits, whether they are of God; because many false prophets have gone out into the world."* (1 John 4:1)

In times when many so-called spiritualist sects have been spreading like wildfire worldwide, I believe more than never that this gift is the weapon to reveal all Satan's plans and strategies, by the power of the Living God, through the Holy Spirit and in the name of the Lord Jesus Christ!

DIFFERENT KINDS OF TONGUES

This gift deals with the ability to speak in different languages after the baptism in the Holy Spirit. According to 1 Corinthians 13:1, there are two kinds of tongues:

Tongues that are unknown to men – the language of angels.

Tongues that are unknown to the person who is speaking and, at times, unknown even to those around him.

When a person speaks in tongues, even though he does not understand the language, he is edifying himself (1 Corinthians 14:4). For this reason, a person that speaks in tongues should be discreet so as not to shock those who are close by and do not understand.

When speaking in tongues many people give in to the flesh and draw attention to themselves by speaking in a loud voice, shouting, and allowing their body to shake all over as if they were full of demons. We should always seek to attract God's attention when speaking in tongues in order to accomplish our goal of being edified. However, when a person is too loud, and diverts other people's attention to himself, causing them to lose concentration, that person is manifesting a demonic selfishness. If a person speaks in tongues to edify himself, why would he speak at a level for others to hear?

The purifying, elevating and transforming effect of speaking in tongues benefits the person who speaks in them. Imagine yourself speaking in a language that is completely unfamiliar to you simply because God had acknowledged your presence and inspired you! When this happens, a person savours personal contact with the Holy Spirit Himself, which in itself is a confirmation of the authenticity of his faith. That was exactly what happened on the Day of Pentecost. It says, *"When the Day of Pentecost had fully come, they were all in one accord in one place. And suddenly there came a sound from heaven, as of a rushing mighty wind, and it filled the whole house where they were sitting. Then there appeared to them divided tongues, as of fire, and one sat upon each of them. And they were all filled with the Holy Spirit and began to speak with other tongues, as the Holy Spirit gave them utterance."*

Acts 2:1-4

It is important to say that not everyone who speaks in tongues is 'in spirit'. Likewise, not everyone who does not speak in tongues is 'out of the spirit'.

We know people who are not yet baptised in the Holy Spirit but whose lives set a better example of holiness than the lives of those who are already baptised. This is because those who are baptised in the Holy Spirit and immediately receive the ability to speak in tongues as evidence of that baptism, do not lose that ability when they make a common mistake. Many times, a person commits a serious sin and even then, when he prays to God, is still able to speak in tongues and edify himself in the Lord Jesus.

I would like to emphasise to all who want to speak in tongues that this gift is definitely not a sign of holiness or consecration. Speaking in tongues aids a person in developing a closer relationship with God.

Interpretation of tongues

The Church of the Lord Jesus will only be edified through tongues if there is someone to interpret them. The apostle Paul went so far as to prohibit the people to speak in tongues in public meetings whenever there was not an interpreter. That was a very reasonable decision (1 Corinthians 14:27,28). God provided the gift of the interpretation of tongues so that His Church could be edified.

When it comes to the body's sense of sight, the eyes are not the only part of the body to benefit, but rather the entire body, just as hearing does not benefit the ears only. This may serve to help us understand how the gifts benefit the members of the Body of Christ as a whole, and how members are assigned tasks. The Spirit of God determines the role of each member and enables him or her to play their part in the functioning of the Body.

In this way the gifts of the Holy Spirit play an important role in helping the Body of Christ, that is, His Church, to win even more souls for the Kingdom of God.

THE DIFFERENCE BETWEEN
THE GIFTS AND THE FRUIT OF THE HOLY SPIRIT

In previous chapters we spoke in particular about the fruit and the gifts of the Holy Spirit. In order to clarify their roles and objectives, we would like to offer the following explanation.

Throughout history serious problems have arisen in the Church of the Lord Jesus Christ, causing scandals that drove many away from the faith, and contributing greatly to the dividing and scattering of the Body of Christ.

Part of this huge problem is the lack of discernment between the fruits and the gifts of the Holy Spirit – one of the primary reasons for the existence of so many different denominations, to such an extent that some consider each other enemies. Yet, in spite of these many troubles and difficulties, the Church of the Lord Jesus continues to experience spontaneous growth. Surely, the power of the Holy Spirit is overcoming the obstacles that Christians themselves have created.

The vast majority has not known how to integrate the fruit and the gifts of the Holy Spirit. For example, there are pastors who are greatly used by the Holy Spirit with regard to spiritual gifts, who forget or simply omit the fruit of the Spirit from their lives. As a minister, he heals the sick, cast out demons, preaches inspired messages and more, however, at home he is a bad example for his children and relatives. In the church he has an appearance of holiness, but behind the scenes, he behaves like an unbeliever. This is extremely common and is one of the reasons that many Christian women are unable to bring their respective husbands and children to the church.

This spiritual imbalance is due to the fact that pastors who are greatly used by the Holy Spirit in their ministries, are set up as examples, and if not careful, tend to think that they are their own masters. They begin to believe that their actions outside the church have the approval of the Holy Spirit. Because the Holy Spirit is using them, they think that they have the right to behave the way they want. Obviously, one thing has nothing to do with the other. If a pastor is used by God to perform miracles for people in need, it is because the Lord wants to reach out to those who are lost, and to show that His Word is true. The pastor is used, but this does not necessarily mean that he is holy before God. God used a donkey when he wanted to speak to Balaam (Numbers 22:28) and ravens to feed the prophet Elijah (1 Kings 17:4), but that does not mean that those animals were pure or holy.

The apostle Paul admonishes us about the gifts and the fruit of the Spirit, saying: *"Though I speak with the tongues of men and of angels* (gift of speaking in tongues), *but have not love, I have become sounding brass or a clanging cymbal. And though I have the gift of prophecy* (gift of prophecy), *and understand all mysteries and all knowledge* (word of wisdom and knowledge), *and though have all faith, so that I could remove mountains* (gift of faith), *but have not love* (fruit of the Spirit), *I am nothing."*

1 Corinthians 13:1,2

According to the apostle Paul, what we are is more important than what we do. In other words, a person's life should manifest love, joy, peace, patience, kindness, goodness, faithfulness, gentleness and self-control not only before God, but also before men and even before demons. In other words, we should live for the Lord Jesus every single day and manifest His glory in this world. This is, and will always be, the supreme desire of God for each one of us. The Lord Jesus said, *"You are the salt of the earth."* (Matthew 5:13)

No one can consider himself a Christian as long as he does not follow the Lord Jesus; likewise, no one can be the salt of the earth as long as his life does not manifest the fruit of the Holy Spirit.

While the fruit of the Spirit reveals our character to the world, the gifts reveal the Spirit to those who hear.

God's desire is that we do His Work, not only for the benefit of His people, but above all, to be living testimonies of the Lord Jesus, as it is written, *"He who says he abides in Him ought to walk just as He walked."* (1 John 2:6)

Books to Build Up Your Faith

THE SUPERNATURAL POWER OF FAITH
Unleash The Supernatural Power of Faith and learn how to make it work for you. You'll be amazed at how much you've been missing!

ARE WE ALL GOD'S CHILDREN?
The biggest and most convincing lie of all times is the belief that we are all God's children.

THE PROFILE OF THE YOUTH OF GOD
In fact the teenage years are the best time to know God and make a covenant with Him. When this happens, everything is possible and defeat is nowhere to be found!

IN THE FOOTSTEPS OF JESUS
In the Footsteps of Jesus will not only help you find the way out of your problems but also teach you how to get the most out of life.

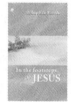

THE FAITH OF ABRAHAM
Read The Faith of Abraham and find out how you can achieve a life of distinction through a close relationship with God.

LIFE MORE ABUNDANT

*In Life More Abundant
Bishop Macedo explains what more
there is to life, as well as the
true meaning of abundance.*

THE HOLY SPIRIT

*The Holy Spirit is a detailed
explanation of the Third Person of the
Holy Trinity as well as a practical guide
to people who truly desire to know Him.*

HOW TO DO THE WORK OF GOD

*How to do the Work of God has the aim to
clarify the position a servant should occupy
before his Master and before the world, as
well as to define his role in the body of the
Church of the Lord Jesus Christ.*

THE REAL MEANING OF THE CROSS

*Your Christian life will
receive strength and inspiration
when you read this book.*

THE CHARACTER OF GOD

*The words of life, wisdom and guidance
contained in The Character of God will
enrich your spiritual life and allow you to
bask in the blessings of divine justice.*

SIN AND REPENTANCE

In this succint but clear booklet, Bishop Macedo helps you understand why you need to rule over sin and teaches you how you can break free from it.

REVIVAL

In this book, you will find a declaration of love for the spiritual growth of the children of God.

CHANGE YOUR LIFE THROUGH YOUR SACRIFICE

Have a deeper understanding of the spiritual meaning of offerings, tithes and sacrifices. But not only that, understand why an offering is much more that just money, and when it has nothing to do with money at all.

GIDEON AND THE 300

You will be amazed at how God does the extraordinary through ordinary people!

Addresses Worldwide

Belgium
>Carnotstraat 152060 Antwerpen
>Helpline: 03/227 31 01

The Netherlands
>Fruitweg 4 2525 KH Den Haag
>Tel.: 070 388 84 42
>Website: www.ukgr.nl
>   www.ikgeloofinwonderen.nl

The Philippines
>Quezon 1 Cinema
>Araneta Center
>(Beside National Bookstore)
>Cubao—Quezon City
>Metro Manila, Philippines
>Helpline: (+63) 2 439 0046

India
>282/681 Thousand Lights
>Mount Road, Chennai 600 006
>Helpline: 091 98412 88171
>   091 44 65449234
>Email: indiauckg@yahoo.com

Hong Kong
>14/F, Tung Hip Commercial Building
>244-252 Des Voeux Road Central
>Sheung Wan, MTR Exit A1
>Hong Kong

The United States of America

New York
1091 Fulton Street
Brooklyn, N.Y. 11238
Toll free number: 888-332-4141

California
1235 Pacific Ave
Long Beach, CA 90813
Helpline: 562-435-3100
Fax: 562-435-3009

4884 Eagle Rock Blvd
Los Angeles, CA 90041
Helpline: 323-550-1551
Email: info@livingfaith.org
Web: www.livingfaith.org

Washington DC
11120 Lockwood Drive
Silver Spring MD 20901-4514

Florida
3501 W. Flagler St.
Miami, FL 33135
Tel: 303 646-1722
      1 800 617-9466

Texas
5150 N. Shepherd Dr
Houston TX 77018
Helpline: +1.888.691.2291

Jamaica
108 Hagley Park Road, Kingston 11
Email: uckgjamaica@hotmail.com
Helpline: 1 (876) 757-8424

South Africa

Temple of Faith
25 Plein Street
Johannesburg 2000
Helpline: 0861 33 0320
Website: www.universalark.co.za

Australia
153 Northumberland Street
Liverpool—2170 NSW
NSW—Australia
Helpline: +61 2 9602 9837
Fax: +61 2 9602 3827
Email: uckg@uckg.org.au
Web: www.uckg.org.au

New Zealand
23 Avenue Road Otahuhu
Auckland—1640
Auckland—New Zealand
Helpline: +649 276 3700
Fax: +649 276 3701
Email: help@uckg.co.nz
Website: www.uckg.co.nz

United Kingdom

UCKG HelpCentre
Rainbow Theatre
232 Seven Sisters Road
Finsbury Park, London N4 3NX
24h Helpline: +44 (0) 20 7686 6000
Website: www.uckg.org
Email: info@uckg.org

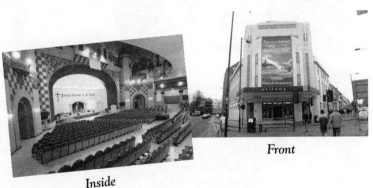

Inside

Front

Reception

Balcony

Counselling Room

Helpline

Boardroom

Baptism pool

Bookshop

Portuguese meeting room

Training Centre

Kids Zone reception

Kids Zone toilet

Foyer

Counselling Room

Delight Cafe

Other churches in the UK

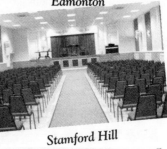

Willesden Green

Edmonton

Plaistow

Stamford Hill

Kilburn

Manchester

Cardiff

Bullring

Bishop Edir Macedo is the founder and leader of the Universal Church of the Kingdom of God, an evangelical church that started in Brazil in 1977 and today is present in more than 100 countries.

Bishop Macedo is not only a respected speaker and lecturer but also a writer with many titles published. Many of them have more than 3 million copies sold.

In the theological field, he stands out among the evangelical ministers in Brazil and in the whole world, having reached the degree of Divinity Doctor (DD), Theology (Th.D), and Christian Philosophy (Ph.D).

His works, as the reader will easily confirm, are of undeniable incentive to the growth in the Word of God.

Unipro

Rio de Janeiro
Estrada Adhemar Bebiano, 3.610
Inhaúma – CEP: 20766-720
Rio de Janeiro – RJ
Tel.: + 55 21 3296-9300
www.universalproducoes.com.br
editora@universalproducoes.com.br

London
FINSBURY PARK
Rainbow Theatre
232 Seven Sisters Road
Finsbury Park London N4 3NX
Tel.: + 44 (0) 20 7686 6000
Fax: + 44 (0) 20 7686 6008
www.uckg.org
info@uckg.org